Early Praise for *Real-World Event Sourcing: Distribute, Evolve, and Scale Your Elixir Applications*

Real-World Event Sourcing flips the script on traditional systems by turning every change into a powerful, immutable event. If you've ever struggled with tangled state logic or scaling challenges, this book is your blueprint for building systems that don't just react—they thrive in complexity.

➤ **Madhu Chavva**
   Vice President of SDK Engineering, GrowthBook

With this book, Kevin Hoffman has given us an informative, practical, and sometimes funny introduction to event sourcing. While the book is focused on building Elixir applications, it is worth a read by anyone interested in learning the fundamentals of event sourcing.

➤ **Russ Olsen**
   President, ROIV

Real-World Event Sourcing

Distribute, Evolve, and Scale Your Elixir Applications

Kevin Hoffman

The Pragmatic Bookshelf

Dallas, Texas

See our complete catalog of hands-on, practical,
and Pragmatic content for software developers:
https://pragprog.com

Sales, volume licensing, and support:
support@pragprog.com

Derivative works, AI training and testing,
international translations, and other rights:
rights@pragprog.com

The team that produced this book includes:

Publisher:	Dave Thomas
COO:	Janet Furlow
Executive Editor:	Susannah Davidson
Development Editor:	Kelly Talbot
Copy Editor:	Corina Lebegioara
Indexing:	Potomac Indexing, LLC
Layout:	Gilson Graphics

ISBN-13: 979-8-88865-106-3
Book version: P1.0—February 2025

Contents

Acknowledgments

Writing a book is hard. Of course, the usual things like syntax and prose, subject mastery, and the ability to distill complex subjects down to small, digestible nuggets are difficult, but I don't think that's the hardest part of writing.

The *real* difficulty is the race between when you finish writing and when your inspiration tank runs dry. At the start of a book project, adrenaline, endorphins, and excitement about the topic keep you fueled. Then, the more you write, the more inspiration you burn. Eventually, as you create text, code samples, and diagrams, you need a way to refuel.

For me, the fuel I needed to finish this book came from my family and coworkers. I couldn't have written this book without the saintly patience and unwavering support of my wife, who, for some reason, continues to put up with me writing book after book. I also couldn't have done this without my daughter, who never failed to ask, "Are you *still* writing your book?"

I'd also like to thank Frances Buontempo, Madhu Chavva, Russ Olsen, Kim Shrier, Stefan Turalski, and everyone else who provided feedback. Your insights and help are greatly appreciated!

Preface

I can still remember the first time I needed event sourcing without knowing it. I'd trapped a handful of players in an elevator in an online multiplayer game. (It was text-based, and it was so long ago we had to share our keyboards with dinosaurs and remnants of the ice age.) My code naively set values on data in direct response to events (like angry players pushing a button). As a result, all it took was a couple of players hitting the button around the same time for them to be trapped in a void halfway between upstairs and downstairs.

At some point, many moons after that disaster, I came to the realization that *everything* is event-sourced. This new understanding brought me joy and returned some of the "awe of learning" to my job again. I wanted to share this joy with everyone but never felt qualified to do so. Finally, after some years (more than I would care to admit) of building software and learning from having failed to build software properly, I have both the joy and the qualifications I've always needed to write this book.

Although I express strong opinions in this book, my goal isn't to make sure you blindly adopt all of them. Rather, its goal is to give you the knowledge, hands-on experience, and information you need to decide whether or not you agree with my opinions and which ones you'll embrace for your next event sourcing project.

This book will teach you how to event-source everything through examples written in Elixir and how to avoid many of the pitfalls common to first attempts at building event-sourced apps. I hope that when you reach the end of it, event sourcing will bring you as much joy as it does for me and you'll go on to build amazing things.

Who Should Read This Book?

This book is for the curious. It's for developers who build app after app and service after service, and who wonder if there's a better way. If you've ever been curious about event sourcing, or wondered if there was a way to create more reliable, testable, and stable systems and maybe even simplify your code at the same time, then this book is for you. If it's always bugged you that an application can give you its current state but can't give you any guarantees about the reliability of that data or even how it came to be, then you'll definitely want to read this book.

The language of choice for this book is Elixir. While some previous knowledge of Elixir will certainly help with running and understanding some of the samples, it isn't strictly required. Many of the samples should be easy enough to read by anyone with exposure to functional programming languages. Some more advanced content leverages GenServer[1] and GenStage,[2] so if you're unfamiliar with those concepts, you may want to read up on them before you progress beyond the fundamentals presented in the first four chapters.

Event sourcing, at least as this book covers it, is primarily a back-end technology. If you're curious about the use of event sourcing in front-end technology, then I suggest checking out languages like Elm[3] and the myriad libraries and tools available for JavaScript/TypeScript like Redux.[4]

About This Book

This book opens with an overview of the fundamental building blocks of event sourcing: aggregates, projectors, notifiers, injectors, and process managers. Once you have a firm grasp of those fundamentals, it's time to start applying them by using libraries, external data stores, persistent streams, and more. Finally, you focus on production by exploring modeling, model discoverability and documentation, testing, security, and preparing for scale. These topics are organized into the following chapters:

Chapter 1: Building Your First Event-Sourced Application
    Whet your appetite with an introduction to event sourcing, what it is, and why we want to use it. Learn about the first building block of event sourcing, the aggregate.

Chapter 2: Separating Read and Write Models
    Learn how to separate the read and write models, what projections are, and when and how to use them.

---

1.   https://hexdocs.pm/elixir/GenServer.html
2.   https://hexdocs.pm/gen_stage/GenStage.html
3.   https://elm-lang.org
4.   https://redux.js.org

Chapter 3: Enforcing Perimeters with Injectors and Notifiers
Interact with external systems and maybe even the "real world" using notifiers and injectors.

Chapter 4: Exploring the Saga of the Process Manager
Model event flows, sequences, and long-running activities using process managers.

Chapter 5: Building Event-Sourced Elixir Apps with Commanded
Learn about Elixir's de facto standard event sourcing library, Commanded.

Chapter 6: Building Resilient Applications with Event Stores
Explore the criteria for choosing an event store and when and why you need them.

Chapter 7: Evolving Event-Sourced Systems
In systems that are supposed to be immutable, learn techniques and rules for how those systems can evolve over time to meet new demands and business requirements.

Chapter 8: Securing Event-Sourced Applications
Security can never be an after-thought. Delve into some of the security concerns that are specific to event-sourced applications.

Chapter 9: Testing Event-Sourced Systems
One of the most powerful benefits of event sourcing is how easily event-sourced applications can be tested. Learn some techniques and patterns for making assertions about event flows.

Chapter 10: Modeling Discoverable Application Domains
We rarely ever build applications in a vacuum. Explore some tools, techniques, and patterns for modeling event-sourced applications and sharing and communicating those models.

Chapter 11: Scaling Up and Out
Finish up your event sourcing journey with a discussion of how scaling event-sourced applications may be different from traditional applications and why that's a good thing.

Appendix 1: The Laws of Event Sourcing
Use this reference as a handy recap of all of the laws of event sourcing that are discussed throughout the book. Of course, it's important to read the book's actual chapters to put them into proper context.

How to Read This Book

This book is neither a reference manual nor a guided tour through a single all-encompassing sample. It's best to read the chapters in order from start to finish. Though some samples may exist on their own without the code from previous chapters, the knowledge, lessons, and rules are all designed to be read in order and to build on the work done earlier.

Conventions Used in This Book

The conventions in this book are generally the same as in any other book from *The Pragmatic Bookshelf*, with a few things specific to this material.

Laws of Event Sourcing

Throughout the book, I'll introduce the *laws of event sourcing*. Each one will appear in an exclamatory block like this one:

All Events Are Immutable and Past Tense

 Every event represents something that actually happened. An event cannot be modified and always refers to something that took place. Modeling the absence of a thing or a thing that didn't actually occur may often seem like a good idea, but doing so can confuse both developers and event processors. Remember that if an error didn't result in some immutable thing happening, it shouldn't be modeled as an event.

While there will be other blocks similar to this, I've made sure that the ones with the exclamation point are the "laws" of event sourcing, which are also presented in the appendix.

Tips and Sidebars

You've already seen the exclamatory blocks of text that explain the laws of event sourcing. You may also occasionally see helpful tips or informative sidebars. Tips look like this:

Helpful Tips

 Helpful tips have the lightbulb icon and provide additional useful or important information. Be sure to pay attention to these as you read the book.

Informative sidebars offer parenthetical or related information that might not be considered part of the book's main core:

Dungeons & Dragons

 I mentioned a random number generator in the code, so as an aside, maybe I should discuss dice-based games like Dungeons & Dragons.

Code Blocks

Code blocks throughout the book generally take the same form, as shown here:

```
defmodule Calculator do
  def add(x, y) do
    x + y
  end

  def mul(x, y) do
    x * y
  end

  def div(x, y) do
    x / y
  end

  def sub(x, y) do
    x - y
  end
end
```

For the most part, the code is formatted the way you might expect Elixir modules to be formatted. But in some cases, the standard Elixir format produces listings that are too long due to excessive carriage returns, too wide for a printed page, and so on. In those cases, we've made our own book-specific formatting choices, and this isn't an oversight but intentional.

Online Resources

As always, the single source of truth for this book and its associated code is the Pragmatic Programmers website.[5] Throughout the book there will be links to GitHub repositories, websites, and other reference materials that complement the book's core text.

Let's Get Started!

Now the fun begins and we can start our event sourcing journey!

---

5.   https://pragprog.com/titles/khpes

## CHAPTER 1

Building Your First Event-Sourced Application

The real world is unpredictable and many scientists would contend that reality itself is merely an illusion—a model that our brain derives from our senses. When we build typical applications, we try and enforce constraints on reality and force it to conform to the software's view of the world. Unfortunately, reality doesn't bend to our will, and, as you'll see throughout this book, the more we embrace the real world and the less we try and contain it, the better off we are. The way we build applications that accept the notion that reality (or application state) is a derived model is through *event sourcing*.

Let's define event sourcing in pragmatic terms. One definition is that we *source* events in order to derive the state of an application. The idea is that the state of any given application is determined by a sequence of immutable events that occurred in the past. As you'll see, events aren't just *a* source of truth, they are *the* one and *only* source of truth. Alternatively, "stateful" applications don't derive their state—state simply *is*. The only source of truth is whatever happens to be in storage at any given time.

Varying degrees of event sourcing conformity exist. The loosest version is *event-driven*, which means that the application reacts to events somewhere internally, but the source of truth in such an application is likely a hybrid of events and persistent state. Phrases like *event-based* and *reactive* also imply that business logic is triggered in response to events somewhere but also probably doesn't follow some of the core rules you'll learn in this book. Only formal event sourcing demands adherence to specific rules. No need to worry about keeping notes on the rules as they're also included in an appendix at the end of the book.

Martin Fowler[1] defines event sourcing more academically as:

> The fundamental idea of Event Sourcing is that of ensuring every change to the state of an application is captured in an event object, and that these event objects are themselves stored in the sequence they were applied for the same lifetime as the application state itself.

Event sourcing is all about deriving meaningful state from *the past*. If you apply an event that occurred in the past to the current state, what you get back is new state. This same pattern is codified as a core tenet of functional programming regarding immutable data and might look something like this defined as an equation:

```
f(state, event) = state'
```

A simple classic example of deriving state from past events is a bank account. If you consider the ledger of transactions to be a list of events (amount withdrawn, amount deposited, and so on) that occurred in the past, then the state (balance) is derived from those transactions.

You'll learn more about why this is such a great event sourcing example later in the book. You'll also pick up a lot more nuance as well as learn a very useful set of event sourcing laws. For now, you've got plenty of information to get started with hands-on exercises.

The Event Sourcing Laws

 I have personally violated each of these laws on past projects and seen the product-breaking consequences firsthand. Some decisions fall into the category of personal or team preference and others are small architectural deviations. But the event sourcing laws are lessons I've specifically gathered over time through retrospectives, post-mortems, and production systems engulfed in flame.

Saying "Hello, Procedural World"

In your learning journey as you read this book and search for extra material, you'll no doubt see architectures and designs that aren't event-driven referred to as *procedural* or *imperative*. Other times these architectures are called *stateful* (or even *state replication*). Naming is hard and the more people involved in a community, the more competing names you find.

So, while *imperative* and *procedural* are not technically accurate as descriptions of non-event-sourced applications, they are often used as shorthand,

---

1.   https://martinfowler.com/eaaDev/EventSourcing.html

so those terms are introduced here. Of all the labels out there, the only ones that provide any accuracy are *event-sourced* and *non-event-sourced*.

The classic "hello world" example prints a little text to the console or screen. You'll explore the messy world of I/O later in Chapter 3, "Enforcing Perimeters with Injectors and Notifiers," on page 27, so for now, let's build something slightly more functional like a calculator. Throughout the book, the samples will be written in Elixir, except when specifically drawing a comparison between how other languages deal with certain concepts or patterns.

To keep it simple to start, let's use the calculator's four basic math operations and not worry about things like divide by zero and overflow errors. In this procedural calculator, four functions are defined in a module. As a developer, you've probably encountered code similar to the following:

```
defmodule Calculator do
  def add(x, y) do
    x + y
  end

  def mul(x, y) do
    x * y
  end

  def div(x, y) do
    x / y
  end

  def sub(x, y) do
    x - y
  end
end
```

Even if this seems like something you've done a thousand times before, go ahead and create this module as calculator.exs. Start up iex and enter c("calculator.exs") to load and compile the module.

Play around with invoking the functions to make sure this all feels familiar and like something you could do blindfolded.

```
iex(1)> Calculator.add(2,2)
4
iex(2)> 8 |> Calculator.add(4) |> Calculator.mul(3)
36
```

In the second command, note how you can chain calculator operations together (but the intermediate result, or running total, is lost). You'll be using this pattern all throughout the book. In a real, physical calculator (the kind they used to make way back before smart phones), state is kept as a running total. You start with 0 and hit the following buttons in sequence, and the screen displays 4:

- 2
- +
- 2
- =

If you then enter +, 6, and then = (or hit Enter), the running total changes to 10. For the most part, this is the default behavior for calculator apps on mobile devices or the ancient physical devices used by our forebears.

Another way to conceptualize this is as a stack. The value 0 is pushed onto the stack during initialization. Then, we push two operands: 2 and 2. When an operator like + is pushed onto the stack, the operator and its operands are popped off and the result, 4, is pushed (as you can see in the following image). The running total is the value sitting at the top of the stack and is used as the first operand to whatever comes next. This way of visualizing operations will help to understand and internalize concepts in the coming chapters, so it's good to start with something easy like a calculator.

Before	**After**
ADD	4
2	
2	

If you guessed that you're going to need to add *state* to this calculator to manage running totals, give yourself a prize.

Building a Stateful and Imperative Calculator

Let's take baby steps toward event sourcing. As with most of life, the journey turns out to be more rewarding than the end goal. In the previous section, you created a stateless, imperative calculator.

An imperative is another word for a command, and we can think of function calls like add, sub, mul, and div as commands. Maintaining state in functional languages is a pretty hefty topic, but a common approach is to have state managed by things like Agents or GenServers and the code that produces state be held in reusable modules or libraries.

Let's refactor the previous module so that instead of specific function calls it accepts commands with the current value (state) in the payload. The return value of each command will be the new value.

Here's a refactored version:

esintro/es_calc_v1.exs
```
defmodule EventSourcedCalculator.V1 do

  def handle_command(%{value: val}, %{cmd: :add, value: v}) do
    %{ value: val + v }
  end

  def handle_command(%{value: val}, %{cmd: :sub, value: v}) do
    %{ value: val - v}
  end

  def handle_command(%{value: val}, %{cmd: :mul, value: v}) do
    %{ value: val * v}
  end

  def handle_command(%{value: val}, %{cmd: :div, value: v}) do
    %{ value: val / v }
  end
end
```

The first parameter to the handle_command function is the state, and the second parameter is the command to process. Load this file up in iex and experiment with some of the functions like in this example:

```
iex(2)> EventSourcedCalculator.V1.handle_command(
...(2)> %{value: 22}, %{cmd: :add, value: 10})
%{value: 32}
iex(3)> EventSourcedCalculator.V1.handle_command(
...(3)> %{value: 5}, %{cmd: :mul, value: 10})
%{value: 50}
```

At first glance, this might seem like a lot of extra ceremony just to perform some basic math. Within the limited context of this problem, it's absolutely more code than is necessary. One of the most common objections to event sourcing, that it requires too much boilerplate, stems from looking at solving trivial problems.

Taken in the context of the larger whole that this book presents, the value of event sourcing will eventually become obvious. Keep that in mind because, before the end of this chapter, you're going to add even more ceremony (but there's a payoff).

Creating Your First Event-Driven Calculator

So far, you've created an imperative calculator and then made it a bit more general-purpose by introducing the concept of a *command*. The command is an instruction to do some work, and the result in the previous example was the result of the actual work.

In the world of event sourcing, this isn't actually how or where work gets done. Remember that events are immutable, and state is only derived from a sequence of events. This means that in the previous code listing we cheated and skipped a step: we combined the role of command and event handler into one.

Let's split out those roles now. The purpose of a command handler is essentially to convert a command into one or more events. State is produced through the application of events. To support this, you'll modify the handle_command functions to return events, and then you'll create handle_event functions that take a previous state and an event to produce a new state.

esintro/es_calc_v2.exs
```
defmodule EventSourcedCalculator.V2 do
  def handle_command(%{value: _val}, %{cmd: :add, value: v}) do
    %{event_type: :value_added, value: v}
  end

  def handle_command(%{value: _val}, %{cmd: :sub, value: v}) do
    %{event_type: :value_subtracted, value: v}
  end

  def handle_command(%{value: _val}, %{cmd: :mul, value: v}) do
    %{event_type: :value_multiplied, value: v}
  end

  def handle_command(%{value: _val}, %{cmd: :div, value: v}) do
    %{event_type: :value_divided, value: v}
  end

  def handle_event(%{value: val},
                   %{event_type: :value_added, value: v}) do
    %{value: val + v}
  end

  def handle_event(%{value: val},
                   %{event_type: :value_subtracted, value: v}) do
    %{value: val - v}
  end
```

```
  def handle_event(%{value: val},
                   %{event_type: :value_multiplied, value: v}) do
    %{value: val * v}
  end

  def handle_event(%{value: val},
                   %{event_type: :value_divided, value: v}) do
    %{value: val / v}
  end
end
```

The first thing to notice is that the command handlers now produce events based on the contents of the command and the current state of the calculator. Command handlers can use their current state to reject invalid commands by not producing any events.

Eventually, working by splitting commands, events, and state becomes second nature. With an imperative function like add(2,2), there's no source of truth. With an immutable event like %{event_type: :value_added, value: 2}, you have an indisputable record that something was added. Please resist the urge to add fields like timestamps or other metadata right now—doing that will get in the way of grasping the big concepts.

As with the other examples, take a moment to poke around and get a *feel* for how this API surface area looks:

```
iex(1)> c("es_calc_v2.exs")
[EventSourcedCalculator.V2]
iex(2)> evt = EventSourcedCalculator.V2.handle_command(
...(2)> %{value: 42}, %{cmd: :add, value: 10})
%{event_type: :value_added, value: 10}
iex(3)> state = EventSourcedCalculator.V2.handle_event(%{value: 9}, evt)
%{value: 19}
```

Pay close attention to what's happening here. An event indicates that *some* value was increased by 10. In the bank ledger domain, this could be a transaction that adds 10 to the running balance. When the example event is applied to a state containing the value 9, the function returns a state containing the value 19. The value in the event passed as state to the event handler wasn't the same value passed as state to the command handler.

As you'll see in a bit, the command handler needs the state to *validate* the command, while the event handler needs the state to produce new state.

Handling Errors by Modeling Failure

Let's take this example to the next step. The code you've written so far is actually fairly brittle. For example, the code can easily be broken with a divide by zero error:

```
iex(4)> evt2 = EventSourcedCalculator.V2.handle_command(%{value: -1},
...(4)>  %{cmd: :div, value: 0})
%{event_type: :value_divided, value: 0}
iex(5)> state2 = EventSourcedCalculator.V2.handle_event(%{value: 9}, evt2)
** (ArithmeticError) bad argument in arithmetic expression
    es_calc_v2.exs:31: EventSourcedCalculator.V2.handle_event/2
```

Modeling errors and failure conditions is an enormous topic covered in detail later in the book, so for now, you'll only handle a couple of easily managed cases. Create a third version of the calculator with the following code:

```
esintro/es_calc_v3.exs
defmodule EventSourcedCalculator.V3 do
  @max_state_value 10_000
  @min_state_value 0

  def handle_command(%{value: val}, %{cmd: :add, value: v}) do
    %{event_type: :value_added,
      value: min(@max_state_value - val, v)}
  end

  def handle_command(%{value: val}, %{cmd: :sub, value: v}) do
    %{event_type: :value_subtracted,
      value: max(@min_state_value, val - v)}
  end

  def handle_command(
        %{value: val},
        %{cmd: :mul, value: v}
      )
      when val * v > @max_state_value do
    {:error, :mul_failed}
  end

  def handle_command(%{value: _val}, %{cmd: :mul, value: v}) do
    %{event_type: :value_multiplied, value: v}
  end

  def handle_command(
        %{value: _val},
        %{cmd: :div, value: 0}
      ) do
    {:error, :divide_failed}
  end

  def handle_command(%{value: _val}, %{cmd: :div, value: v}) do
    %{event_type: :value_divided, value: v}
  end
```

```elixir
  def handle_event(
        %{value: val},
        %{event_type: :value_added, value: v}
      ) do
    %{value: val + v}
  end

  def handle_event(
        %{value: val},
        %{event_type: :value_subtracted, value: v}
      ) do
    %{value: val - v}
  end

  def handle_event(
        %{value: val},
        %{event_type: :value_multiplied, value: v}
      ) do
    %{value: val * v}
  end

  def handle_event(
        %{value: val},
        %{event_type: :value_divided, value: v}
      ) do
    %{value: val / v}
  end

  def handle_event(%{value: _val} = state, _) do
    state
  end
end
```

A couple of highlights here are that this code enforces an upper and lower bound on the calculator state. Code like this will accept commands that could overflow values by modifying the changed amounts. In the preceding code, the @max_state_value module constant limits the value on the event.

Let's see how this new code behaves:

```
iex(2)> EventSourcedCalculator.V3.handle_command(
...(2)> %{value: 9500}, %{cmd: :add, value: 650})
%{event_type: :value_added, value: 500}
```

This is the first new feature: the command requested that the value 650 be added, but due to the ceiling implementation, only 500 was added. This may seem like a small detail now, but this kind of behavior will be critically important later. Command handlers should never be considered as merely "blindly converting a command into an event that occurred in the past." Put another way, a command represents a request for something to happen, an event represents what *actually* happened, and the two will only ever look identical in the simplest of cases.

Let's see what happens when you try to divide by zero:

```
iex(3)> EventSourcedCalculator.V3.handle_command(
...(3)> %{value: 9500}, %{cmd: :div, value: 0})
{:error, :divide_failed}
```

This is another subtle but important detail. The command was rejected outright, so the code returned an error type of :divide_failed. Since nothing happened as a result of this command, *no event was emitted*. Sometimes it may seem useful to emit an "error event," but that has many consequences. When to emit error events and when to simply reject commands is something that will be covered throughout the book as you model different domains.

This brings up the first event sourcing law: "All Events Are Immutable and Past Tense."

All Events Are Immutable and Past Tense

 Every event represents something that actually happened. An event cannot be modified and always refers to something that took place. Modeling the absence of a thing or a thing that didn't actually occur may often seem like a good idea, but doing so can confuse both developers and event processors. Remember that if an error didn't result in some immutable thing happening, it shouldn't be modeled as an event.

To not break this rule, you need to not store an event for command validation failures. While guidelines for when to emit events for failures are hotly debated, my personal opinion distilled from much suffering is that validation failures aren't events.

The critical aspect here is that the event handler isn't where validation happens; validation happens in a command handler. After all, if the thing already occurred, how can we go back in time to validate it?

Chapter 11, "Modeling and Discovering Application Domains," on page 139, goes into more detail and provides tips and tricks that will help with modeling failure and other edge cases.

Of course, repeatedly handling commands and applying the resulting events while still maintaining an intermediate result looks an awful lot like a *fold*. In functional programming, a fold is a higher-order function that performs a recursive operation on some list of data, progressively building up a single return value. Another form of a fold is a *reduce*, which, as the name implies, *reduces* a list of elements into a single element. Operations like summing the numbers in a list or producing a final balance from a list of ledger items can all be represented as a fold.

Indeed, you could say that the state of any event-sourced component can be produced by *folding* a function over the event stream. Let's look at how to do that with the sample you've been building so far. Make sure the es_calc_v3.exs file has been compiled and EventSourcedCalculator.V3 imported.

```
iex(3)> cmds = [%{cmd: :add, value: 10},
...(3)> %{cmd: :add, value: 50}, %{cmd: :div, value: 0},
...(3)> %{cmd: :add, value: 2}]
[
  %{cmd: :add, value: 10},
  %{cmd: :add, value: 50},
  %{cmd: :div, value: 0},
  %{cmd: :add, value: 2}
]
iex(4)> initial = %{value: 0}
%{value: 0}
iex(5)> cmds |> List.foldl(initial,
...(5)>   fn cmd, acc -> handle_event(acc, handle_command(acc,cmd)) end)
%{value: 62}
iex(6)>
```

Now, having worked through the exercises in this chapter on your own, hopefully, you received the payoff of a nice fresh hit of dopamine. At this point, you can declare a sequence of commands that you wish to send to a calculator. You can then fold that list of commands by passing the event produced by the handle_command function (if any) to the handle_event function. The preceding code can be refactored to use more of the pipeline operator, but this syntax is hopefully a bit more easily read.

It's important that you know what happened to the event produced by %{cmd: :div, value: 0}. As you know, this produces a failure event. Recall the following code from the third version of the calculator:

```
def handle_event(%{value: _val} = state, _) do
  state
end
```

This fallthrough matches any event that the calculator doesn't handle. The calculator doesn't explicitly handle the :divide_failed error, so this function picks that up. This brings up the second law of event sourcing: "Applying a Failure Event Must Always Return the Previous State."

Applying a Failure Event Must Always Return the Previous State

 Any attempt to apply a bad, unexpected, or explicitly modeled failure event to an existing state must always return the existing state. Failure events should only indicate that a failed thing occurred in the past, not command rejections.

No matter what happens during the processing of an event, a failure during processing or an event that indicated a failure must always return the state current at the time of processing. This rule is actually what makes an event *stream* possible. If processing an event could break the stream, event sourcing wouldn't work.

Working with Event Sourcing Aggregates

In this chapter, you've actually been building what Martin Fowler[2] calls an *aggregate* without labeling it as such. At a conceptual level, an aggregate is a *single*, uniquely identifiable entity that has state, validates commands, and emits events.

Every aggregate must have a unique identifier or key. This differentiates one aggregate from another within the same event stream. By way of example, consider a group or a class called BankAccount. Given a stream of ledger events, the key that differentiates one aggregate from another might be the key field account_number. In this case, you can say that there's an aggregate type called BankAccount, and one aggregate (or aggregate instance, depending on where you get your lexicon from) might be for account_number=1235 while another aggregate instance might be for account_number=6789. In technical terms, aggregates only exist when paired with their unique IDs or keys.

Depending on which book or blog post you read, you may see examples of internal aggregate state being shared and used for user-facing queries. As you'll learn in this book, *aggregate state is not to be shared and not meant for external consumption*. In the next chapter, you'll learn about a special kind of state optimized for external consumption called the *projection*.

An event sourcing aggregate has the following required characteristics:

- Validates incoming commands and returns one or more events
- Applies events to state to produce new state
- Application of events and commands is pure and referentially transparent

---

2.   https://martinfowler.com/bliki/DDD_Aggregate.html

The first two bullets seem straightforward, but what do *pure* and *referentially transparent* mean?

By pure, we mean that the function can have no side effects. A side effect is something that happens to the world outside the function and isn't captured in the return value. If a function has no side effects, then it can be referentially transparent, always producing the same results for the same input.

This is where we lose a lot of potential users of event sourcing. This is the first set of rules that people think is either too hard or too demanding. Fear not because you'll learn techniques and patterns that not only alleviate these concerns but also embrace the limitations.

Wrapping Up

Congratulations! You've converted an imperative calculator into an event-sourced one, and you've taken the first step on the exciting journey toward thinking like an "eventhead" (I just made this word up and cannot be held responsible for people's reactions if you attempt to use it in public). At this point, many developers prefer to take this initial bit of knowledge, open the door, and jump out of the airplane without a parachute.

It might be tempting to think that there's nothing more to know and to start building a new event-sourced application right now, but building before learning the techniques and consequences for patterns may result in disappointment, or worse, writing a heated blog post that complains about the failures of event sourcing. By all means, tinker but also keep reading.

In the next chapter, we'll continue building your practical event sourcing knowledge by talking about the separation of read and write models via projectors.

## CHAPTER 2

Separating Read and Write Models

Now that you've started your event sourcing journey by learning about aggregates and building simple examples, next, you'll learn about another building block, which involves separating an application's read and write models. The concept of separating the read model from the write model is nothing new. Databases have supported views as a separate read model since the dawn of time, allowing the creation of customized sets of data designed to answer specific queries. Sometimes this is just a shortcut for another query, while other times a *materialized view* (such as a denormalized table or even a simple key-value store) stores a totally separate copy of data in anticipation of queries.

The concept of materialized views and the separation of models translates quite well to event sourcing. You've already encountered the write model: the immutable event log and aggregate state. This chapter focuses on *projections*, which are the event sourcing counterparts to the read model and materialized views.

Justifying Model Separation

In a traditional application, you might store data in tables and then link all that data together with keys. When your application wants to display a list of users, it can query the user table and join it with the address table, then join that with a ZIP code table, and so on. There's nothing inherently wrong with this, but you're out of luck if you need to know *how* or *when* a person's address became their current one. Without an event log, that information doesn't exist.

You need both the event log (*write model*) and the user, address, ZIP code, billing, preferences, and other data (*read model*). But using the same data structure for both is at best impractical, and at worst impossible. If you had to query the entire history of the world from the event log every time you needed to know a user's current address, your application would eventually grind to a halt.

Simply separating the data that supports queries from the data that supports logic is rarely good enough. If the *shapes* of your write model and read model are similar, you typically run into performance problems. In the preceding example, if you have to use a handful of SQL joins every time a client needs data, this can potentially slow your system down and cause unnecessary delays in the client.

The key is to anticipate your consumers. You should know the way your users will interact with your application (or at least how you expect them to) and the information they'll need. You can design your read model so that the data required to answer any query is pregenerated, anxiously awaiting an incoming query. Of course, applications and the needs of consumers change, but the use of projections makes it easy to grow and adapt the read model along with those needs. Clients will always have to query data, but with projections (or generated read models), the goal is to make those queries executable in a fixed (O(1)) time.

As you'll see throughout this chapter, taking incoming information from the write model and using it to pregenerate data in anticipation of consumer queries is at the heart of event sourcing and the concept of projections.

As with many aspects of event sourcing, the effort involved in this might seem like overkill for the "hello world" class of problems, but once you start solving problems at a real-world scale, anticipating user queries not only enhances performance but for many applications is also simply mandatory.

Building Your First Projection

The bank account ledger example is one of the easiest to build and understand in event sourcing, so let's start there. In this exercise, you'll build a projection for a bank account balance. In more formal terms, you'll build a *projector* that takes data from events in the event log and stores that data in a read model projection, which can then be queried by consumers.

A projector is a piece of code responsible for producing read model data for consumption by one or more parties. For this sample, the projector is AccountBalance and the projection is a piece of data containing the most up-to-date balance for a given account. As with aggregates, projections have *keys* that allow you to differentiate one from another. The bank ledger example is easy because it has an obvious key: the account number.

Let's start with the client API for the projector and then move on to the implementation details. Assume that you want to be able to perform the following tasks:

```
iex(1)> Projectors.AccountBalance.apply_event(%{event_type: :amount_deposited,
...(1)> account_number: "NEWACCOUNT", value: 12})
:ok
iex(2)> Projectors.AccountBalance.lookup_balance("NEWACCOUNT")
{:ok, 12}
```

In this code, an event (:amount_deposited) is applied to a projector, and then the projected balance is available for query. A subtle point here is that the apply_event function doesn't accept a key separate from the event. This is to avoid accidentally applying an event to the wrong projection. You don't want to apply the deposit event to OLDACCOUNT if the value of account_number on the event is NEWACCOUNT. This brings up another law of event sourcing: "All Data Required for a Projection Must Be on the Events."

All Data Required for a Projection Must Be on the Events

 The event is the *only* source of truth. If code allows a different piece of information to be supplied as a parameter that contradicts information on the event, you can corrupt an entire event stream. As such, all keys, metadata, and payload data must come from events and nowhere else. This is often one of the hardest laws to follow but the penalties for breaking it can be subtle and disastrous.

Implicit information can also be used by projectors. For example, in many cases, especially when building things like rolling averages, the projector may need to make use of event counts or previously calculated data. If you're thinking that previously calculated data is data not on events, and so it violates the rule you just learned, that's natural. The distinction is subtle and pedantic, but projectors can maintain their own internal state, also derived from the event log. The key is that this behavior is still referentially transparent, and given the same event log, a projector will always produce the same output.

In this chapter, you'll be creating projectors as GenServers that manage their projections as in-memory data. Later in Chapter 12, "Scaling Out the Event Sourcing Building Blocks," on page 159, you'll get to dive deep into techniques for dealing with distributed, persistent, highly available projections.

But for now, let's focus on simple projections and create an empty scaffold for the GenServer:

```elixir
defmodule Projectors.AccountBalance do
  use GenServer
  require Logger

  def start_link(account_number) do
    GenServer.start_link(
      __MODULE__,
      account_number,
      name: via(account_number))
  end

  @impl true
  def init(account_number) do
    {:ok, %{balance: 0, account_number: account_number}}
  end

  defp via(account_number) do
    {:via, Registry,
      {Registry.AccountProjectors, account_number}}
  end
end
```

This is enough to call Projectors.AccountBalance.start_link("my_account") and get back a pid. This server maintains a projection that has the account number and the current balance. In order to trigger this server to update the balance, let's add some functions for the application of events. Note that since this process is using a named registry (Registry.AccountProjectors), we can't call start_link until after we've created the registry, either manually or by adding it to the application's supervision tree.

```elixir
def apply_event(%{account_number: account} = event)
    when is_binary(account) do
  case Registry.lookup(Registry.AccountProjectors, account) do
    [{pid, _}] ->
      apply_event(pid, event)
    _ ->
      Logger.debug(
        "Attempt to apply event to non-existent account, starting projector")
      {:ok, pid} = start_link(account)
      apply_event(pid, event)
  end
end

def apply_event(pid, event) when is_pid(pid) do
  GenServer.cast(pid, {:handle_event, event})
end

@impl true
def handle_cast({:handle_event, evt}, state) do
  {:noreply, handle_event(state, evt)}
end
```

```
def handle_event(%{balance: bal} = s,
                  %{event_type: :amount_withdrawn, value: v}) do
  %{s | balance: bal - v}
end

def handle_event(%{balance: bal} = s,
                  %{event_type: :amount_deposited, value: v}) do
  %{s | balance: bal + v}
end

def handle_event(%{balance: bal} = s,
                  %{event_type: :fee_applied, value: v}) do
  %{s | balance: bal - v}
end
```

A couple of interesting things are going on here. The first is that if an event arrives for an account that doesn't yet have a running projector, the code starts one with an initial balance of 0. There will always be one server per account, each maintaining its own projection. An Elixir process registry is used to manage the list of all projectors, keyed on the account number.

Next, let's add some code to allow consumers to query the balance of any given account:

```
def lookup_balance(account_number) when is_binary(account_number) do
  with [{pid, _}] <-
    Registry.lookup(Registry.AccountProjectors, account_number) do
    {:ok, get_balance(pid) }
  else
    _ ->
      {:error, :unknown_account}
  end
end

def get_balance(pid) do
  GenServer.call(pid, :get_balance)
end

@impl true
def handle_call(:get_balance, _from, state) do
  {:reply, state.balance, state}
end
```

The registry[1] (note you'll have to start this explicitly via start_link, as shown in the next example, or through a supervision tree) makes for an ideal way of locating the process responsible for the account balance projection for a given account. If there's no running projector, then the balance query will return {:error, :unknown_account}.

---

1.   https://hexdocs.pm/elixir/1.12/Registry.html

With all of this in the module, exercise what you've built so far:

```
iex(1)> {:ok, _} = Registry.start_link(keys: :unique,
...(1)> name: Registry.AccountProjectors)
{:ok, #PID<0.304.0>}
iex(2)> c("balance_projector.exs")
[Projectors.AccountBalance]

iex(3)> Projectors.AccountBalance.apply_event(
...(3)>   %{event_type: :amount_deposited,
...(3)>   account_number: "NEWACCOUNT", value: 12})

12:50:45.426 [debug] Attempt to apply event to non-existent account,
   starting projector
:ok

iex(4)> Projectors.AccountBalance.apply_event(
...(4)>   %{event_type: :amount_deposited,
...(4)>   account_number: "NEWACCOUNT", value: 30})
:ok
iex(5)> Projectors.AccountBalance.lookup_balance("NEWACCOUNT")
{:ok, 42}
iex(6)> Projectors.AccountBalance.lookup_balance("DOESNOTEXIST")
{:error, :unknown_account}
```

That's all there is to it! The state-updating aspect of projectors is easy. It doesn't take much effort to perform some basic business logic and store the result. In real applications, instead of manually calling apply_event, you would likely see a dispatch or routing system that funnels events from a stream through projectors.

As you'll see in the more advanced exercises, the more challenging part of projectors is designing the events and projections and working within the many constraints enforced by event sourcing.

Aggregate State vs. Projections

 Aggregates maintain their own state. This state must be considered private and is only ever used to validate commands sent to the aggregate and populate outgoing events. This differs from projections, which are designed to be shared, communal views accessible to any consumer that knows how to find and interpret them. In simple cases, aggregate state and projection data may be indistinguishable, but resist the temptation to combine them or violate role boundaries because doing so can remove the predictable and repeatable aspects of an event-sourced system.

Let's move on to a more sophisticated, and realistic, example.

Projecting a Leaderboard

Leaderboards are an ideal example of projections. They take a long stream of data and distill it down to a very small bit of summarized information. Most leaderboards of any size can take prohibitively long to generate, which reinforces the need for a separation of read and write models.

Let's consider a video game in which the goal is to kill zombies. You want to generate a leaderboard that shows the top 10 most prolific zombie slayers of all time. To produce this on demand, you would have to query the entire history of zombie kills from the game's release day until the present day.

The following is an example of the leaderboard you'll generate for this game that shows the top 10 zombie killers of all time.

#	Player	Kills
1	zomb0_masher_31	32,766
2	Boylur Plait	32,001
3	Deploy Jenkins	29,352
4	Kode Friez	29,001
5	Sir Emony	28,457
6	Dubble Tap	25,321
7	Kardeeo	23,275
8	Headshot McGee	21,321
9	Brains-n-Yogurt	18,703
10	how_do_i_play_this	15,321

Table 1—Top 10 Zombie Killers of All Time

Before you can rank the top 10 killers, you'll need to maintain a running total of the kill count for each player. This comes in handy because this intermediate projection can be used to display a kill count on a number of game status screens. Once you have these totals, you can sort them in descending order and cut the list off at 10.

Let's build a leaderboard projector using the same GenServer pattern as before. You can create this in a single file called leaderboard_projector.exs.

chap2/leaderboard_projector.exs
```elixir
defmodule Projectors.Leaderboard do
  use GenServer
  require Logger

  # Client API
  def start_link() do
    GenServer.start_link(__MODULE__, nil)
  end

  def apply_event(pid, evt) do
    GenServer.cast(pid, {:handle_event, evt})
  end

  def get_top10(pid) do
    GenServer.call(pid, :get_top10)
  end

  def get_score(pid, attacker) do
    GenServer.call(pid, {:get_score, attacker})
  end

  # Callbacks
  @impl true
  def init(_) do
    {:ok, %{scores: %{}, top10: []}}
  end

  @impl true
  def handle_call({:get_score, attacker}, _from, state) do
    {:reply, Map.get(state.scores, attacker, 0), state}
  end

  @impl true
  def handle_call(:get_top10, _from, state) do
    {:reply, state.top10, state}
  end

  @impl true
  def handle_cast(
        {:handle_event, %{event_type: :zombie_killed, attacker: att}},
        state
      ) do
    new_scores = Map.update(state.scores, att, 1, &(&1 + 1))
    {:noreply, %{state | scores: new_scores, top10: rerank(new_scores)}}
  end

  defp rerank(scores) when is_map(scores) do
    scores
    |> Map.to_list()
    |> Enum.sort(fn {_k1, val1}, {_k2, val2} -> val1 >= val2 end)
    |> Enum.take(10)
  end
end
```

This should all seem straightforward. The GenServer here is maintaining two pieces of information: a map of player names to their lifetime total kill count and a top 10 list. Recreating the top 10 list after each event means consumers don't have to do any work or wait for a query to finish to read this leaderboard; it's already there waiting for them. This leaderboard is still considered a single projection, even though it's maintaining intermediate data.

If part of your mind is screaming, "but that won't scale!", try to suppress that reaction for now, as you'll learn how to deal with this in Chapter 12, "Scaling Out the Event Sourcing Building Blocks," on page 159.

Projecting Advanced Leaderboards

Projecting a standard top 10 leaderboard is easy enough, but what happens when the requirements get a little more tricky? It's at this point that it can be tempting to start violating the laws of event sourcing. A more advanced leaderboard might be one where you're displaying the top 10 killers *this week*. Here's an example of that type of leaderboard showing this week's top 10 zombie hunters.

#	Player	Kills
1	Kode Friez	931
2	Boylur Plait	751
3	Deploy Jenkins	750
4	zomb0_masher_31	722
5	Sir Emony	721
6	Dubble Tap	650
7	Kardeeo	601
8	Headshot McGee	580
9	Brains-n-Yogurt	512
10	how_do_i_play_this	301
41	-> Pragmatic Player (you)	87

Table 2—This Week's Top 10 Zombie Killers

Some ways of solving this problem are hard, and others are deceptively easy. Before you try to solve any event sourcing problem that seems difficult or impossible on the surface, *see if you can model your way out of the problem.*

If you need to retrieve the top 10 killers within the past seven days, then you'll need to be able to query each player's total within the past seven days. It might be tempting to think the answer here is to run some kind of database query and table join on time-filtered rows, which isn't very "*projection-y*".

Without access to the wall clock (remember never to query real-world time in event sourcing), you can't query up until now(). You'd have to grab the timestamp from the most recent event and then work backward from there for seven days. This could be regenerated every time a zombie kill event comes in.

Here's where it might be more useful to model your way out of the problem. Have you ever noticed how the weekly leaderboards for many games aren't based on the previous seven days but are actually based on a fixed week? The leaderboards often reset on Sunday or Monday. Achievements, trials, and many other things also reset on a fixed schedule. While games probably have countless reasons for this, one might be that it's easier to manage data that way.

The two solutions might seem the same, but a leaderboard that resets to 0 on Sunday is *significantly* easier to deal with than a leaderboard that always contains a sliding window of the past seven days' worth of kills. If your game system (outside the boundaries of your event-sourced perimeter) simply injects a :week_completed event into the stream, then your projectors can just wipe out weekly data. To do this, add the following handle_cast function to the previous GenServer.

```
@impl true
def handle_cast(
      {:handle_event, %{event_type: :week_completed}},
      _state
    ) do
  {:noreply, %{scores: %{}, top10: []}}
end
```

With an event handler for :week_completed, you can wipe out all weekly leaderboards as well as easily archive those weekly leaderboards so that you can maintain a history. Now you can query last week's kills, the week before, and so on—all without having to scan the event stream on demand. It cannot be restated enough that the easiest path out of a seemingly difficult event sourcing problem may be to model the situation differently.

Crossing the event sourcing hard boundary between the real world and the pure functional world isn't something to be done lightly, which is why Chapter 3, "Enforcing Perimeters with Injectors and Notifiers," on page 27, goes into detail on that very concept.

Understanding Projectors and CQRS

CQRS stands for *Command Query Responsibility Segregation* and was originally coined by Greg Young. Depending on which definition, book, or website you're reading, this can either be described as adjacent to, or within, the concept of event sourcing. Occasionally, you'll even see people (incorrectly) treat CQRS and event sourcing as the same thing. I'm not a fan of the word *segregation*, so I often use *separation* instead. At a high level, CQRS states that the mutation (commands) and the read model (queries) are isolated from each other, and the application takes on a more vertical design rather than the classical n-tier or horizontal architectural style. As a subset of event sourcing, CQRS is required to be event-sourced but not the reverse. Aggregates deal with the command side by validating and then emitting events, while projectors deal with the query side of CQRS.

Wrapping Up

In this chapter, you've worked with another fundamental building block of event sourcing, the projector. Projectors handle events and produce views of data designed specifically with consumers in mind. In contrast, aggregates also process events to produce state, but that state is internal. One important thing to take away from this chapter is that, more often than not, you'll be able to solve difficult problems by coming up with a different way to model events rather than resorting to "giving up" on event sourcing and doing things in the classic, imperative style. Next, you're going to learn how to safely interact with external systems with injectors and notifiers.

## CHAPTER 3

Enforcing Perimeters with Injectors and Notifiers

So far, you've learned that an aggregate applies a function to a command to produce events. That same aggregate also applies another function to a stream of events to produce the internal state used for validating those commands. You've also seen that a projector takes a stream of events and produces query-friendly data views. In this chapter, you'll get to experiment with two additional event sourcing building blocks: the *injector* and the *notifier*.

In pure functional programming terms, interaction with external systems is considered *impure* because those interactions are *side effects*. Different languages handle side effects in different ways, but in functional programming languages, I/O is usually treated as something to be managed, controlled, and kept clear of the "pure" part of a program.

Using the injector and notifier is an exercise in managing event sourcing side effects. The injector and notifier provide a way to integrate with systems that aren't event-sourced, aren't under our control, or both. Using the injector and notifier patterns lets us manage side effects without affecting the pure functional nature of the rest of the system.

Handling Input and Output in an Event-Sourced World

As you've learned the building blocks in the first chapters of the book, you've also picked up a few rules worth going over again to help you understand why aggregates and projectors exist. One is that neither projectors nor aggregates are allowed to access the "wall clock," which stems from the law that all data required must be on the events. If an aggregate's state can be different after applying an event first thing in the morning versus late at night, then it's no longer predictable and repeatable as required by aggregates. You'll also see how accessing a real clock can ruin replays in Chapter 6, "Building Resilient Applications with Persistent Events," on page 81.

The other event sourcing law is that all events are immutable and exist in the past. Based on what you've learned so far, the flow of data through an event-sourced system looks like the following diagram, which might make it easy to assume that aggregates are the only source of events in a system.

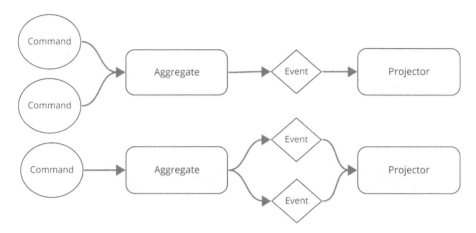

You've seen that an event can only represent a value at the time it was created and never change. So how do we handle the real world, where a value might be changing continuously or continually, such as the outside temperature, or a stock price?

We need a way to allow event-sourced systems to react to things that came from the unstructured and messy "real world," as well as push events back out into that same world. To get started, let's look at the input side of things.

Reacting to Injected Events

The code to react to an injected event is easy: just handle the event. The trick, as with all things event-sourced, is how to design the model properly. When evaluating whether something should be injected and *where* it should be injected, you can ask these questions:

- Does the external event represent something important to the components in your system?

- Does the event occur without the aid of an internal command?

- Does the occurrence of the event have meaning beyond the ephemeral state?

- Does the occurrence of the event also affect the state of an aggregate in your system?

If an external event occurs without the aid of a command in your system but its occurrence signifies something important that can impact projections, then this event should be injected. Events to be injected are the ones that represent something that impacts more than the ephemeral state.

For example, if you don't care about the history of whether a smart bulb was on or off, and the only thing that really matters is whether it's currently lit, then maybe the external smart bulb events don't need to be injected because these events don't impact any of your managed state. But, if you have an IoT motion sensor set up for intrusion detection, then the history of motion detection events is indeed something that should be injected by writing events to the log.

Once you've decided to inject an event, you'll need to make sure that it's written to the event log the same way all of your other events are. This means that any of your aggregates, process managers, or projectors can react to this external event.

Notifying External Consumers

Notifying external consumers is also pretty easy. To create a notifier, you create something that's listening on some portion of the event stream for relevant events. The notifier then does whatever data massaging is necessary (which can include querying from projections) and then emits some stimuli out into the real world.

One of the most common examples of this is a notifier listening for events indicating business process failure. When it encounters those, it can send messages to a Slack channel, email an operations mailbox, or interact with an application's API.

Here are a few more common examples of notifiers:

- Submit a label request to a third-party shipper when an order has been placed
- Email a customer when the status of an order changes
- Publish federated chat messages from internal chats to an external source
- Invoke webhooks in response to certain events

You also shouldn't use notifiers to trigger further internal processing. For example, if someone signs up for notifications for a certain flight, that may trigger the creation of a flight monitor Elixir process or a message broker subscription. This isn't the job of a notifier, but instead is the responsibility of a *process manager*, which you'll explore in Chapter 4, "Exploring the Saga of the Process Manager," on page 47.

You also shouldn't use notifiers to trigger further internal processing. For example, if someone signs up for notifications for a certain flight, that may trigger the creation of a flight monitor Elixir process or a message broker subscription. This isn't the job of a notifier, but instead is the responsibility of a *process manager*, which you'll explore in Chapter 4, "Exploring the Saga of the Process Manager," on page 47.

Notifiers *must never* place events or commands back onto the internal stream; they can only subscribe internally and emit externally. Because of how simple the code often looks for these small components, it's tempting to conflate roles, but resist the temptation to do that. You'll be grateful that you kept the roles clear and isolated once you get into building much larger applications.

Introducing Cloud Events

Whether injecting, emitting, or internally processing, a number of pieces of information are typically required for every event. Events need a timestamp, a type, and typically things like a unique ID, an origin, and a handful of other metadata. If our event store can ensure things like global ordering, regular timestamps are sufficient. If not, then in a widely distributed system we might need to look into things like CRDTs (conflict-free replicated data types)[1] or Lamport[2] clocks (concepts outside the scope of this book). We're going to be using tools and apps throughout the book that won't require us to do things the "hard way" with CRDTs.

Having a common way of transmitting events over the wire means that many disparate systems can all participate in the same set of event streams. If an agreed-upon canonical format exists, then, if systems need their own private formats, writing converters is also fairly straightforward.

One such attempt at a canonical event format is Cloud Events.[3] Cloud Events is a Cloud Native Computing Foundation open source project. The specifica-

---

1. https://en.wikipedia.org/wiki/Conflict-free_replicated_data_type
2. https://en.wikipedia.org/wiki/Lamport_timestamp
3. https://cloudevents.io

tions for the event representation format can all be found on their website. For this book, wherever cloud events are used, the JSON format is preferred. Other representation formats are available for Cloud Events, but JSON is a nice compromise between human and machine readability as well as portable utility.

The Cloud Events specification defines a header format (often referred to as an "envelope" in some circles) for each event. Some of the fields in the header include the following:

- specversion—The version of Cloud Events to which this event conforms

- type—A fully qualified name of the event type, for example, org.thisbook.that-sample.this_event

- source—A free-form identifier indicating the originator of the event

- id—A unique identifier for the event. See the specification for rules regarding what constitutes a valid ID

- datacontenttype—A mime type that indicates the type of data that can be found in the data field

- time—An ISO 8601 string formatted timestamp

- data—The actual payload

Having fields like type, source, and time on events that will be persisted in a durable (and quarriable) event log can prove invaluable. For the rest of the book, unless the sample requires some other format, events will be managed according to the Cloud Events JSON specification.

Let's write a quick utility function that generates a cloud event from an arbitrary Elixir map (this code uses the Cloudevents library found on hex.pm):

```elixir
defp new_cloudevent(type, data) do
  %{
    "specversion" => "1.0",
    "type" => "org.book.flighttracker.#{String.downcase(type)}",
    "source" => "radio_aggregator",
    "id" => UUID.uuid4(),
    "datacontenttype" => "application/json",
    "time" => DateTime.utc_now() |> DateTime.to_iso8601(),
    "data" => data
  }
  |> Cloudevents.from_map!()
  |> Cloudevents.to_json()
end
```

This will produce JSON that looks similar to the following (data elided for readability):

```
{
    "specversion" : "1.0",
    "type" : "org.book.flighttracker.aircraft_identified",
    "source" : "radio_aggregator",
    "subject": null,
    "id" : "0f749a4f-6f2c-4301-9521-21a9459080b4",
    "time" : "2024-04-05T17:31:00Z",
    "data" : { ... }
}
```

Building a Flight Tracker with Injection and Notification

One of the best aspects of event sourcing is that it's *fun*. As you've discovered already, the code to write notifiers and injectors is trivial—they're simply event handlers and event emitters. The trick with event sourcing I/O is, as with so many problems, proper modeling. To start modeling injection and notification, and hopefully have a lot of fun with a sample application, let's build a flight tracker.

This flight tracker will capture incoming events from a real-time flight data source and inject them into the internal event stream. You'll set up a notifier to send notifications to a user when changes happen to a flight they're interested in and a projector that will store the most current information on a per-flight basis. All of this is actually remarkably easy to set up in your own home with a small antenna and a USB dongle, though for this example test data is provided so you don't need to struggle with the hardware.

Airplanes flying in accordance with regulations are constantly emitting data in a format called ADS-B,[4] which stands for *Automatic Dependent Surveillance-Broadcast*. This information can be picked up by other nearby planes, traffic control, and home hobbyists with antennas.

Anyone within range of these radio signals, like a home or even a laptop with an antenna, can pick up the signals, decode them, and use them to obtain real-time information like flight call signs, location, altitude, velocity, and more. A number of affordable ways to do this exist, but the easiest is to use something called a *software defined radio* (SDR). For more information on this family of devices, you'll want to do some research on one of the most popular and affordable SDRs, the RTL-SDR.[5] The RTL-SDR website has all

---

4. https://www.faa.gov/air_traffic/technology/adsb
5. https://www.rtl-sdr.com

the information you need to get a radio dongle and antenna, but you don't need to worry about antennas or other hardware to work with this chapter. Sample files are provided to emulate the signal data.

In the application you're going to build, you'll be taking the various ADS-B messages and *injecting* them into the application's internal event stream. From there, these events will be used to populate projections like the current location of any given flight. Finally, you'll create a (fake) notifier that sends a notification to an interested party whenever relevant events happen. Think of this like creating an alert on your mobile app to give you real-time updates on your upcoming flight.

The message and event flow through the system looks like the following diagram:

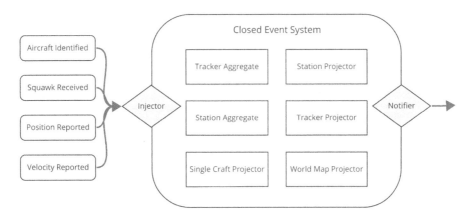

As indicated by the diagram, you'll need to be able to inject the following events:

- Aircraft Identified
- Squawk Received
- Position Reported
- Velocity Reported

Each of the injected events will be converted into the Cloud Events JSON format so that the event stream has a relatively standard structure and there's a reliable way to distinguish one event type from another. So far, the code samples have been either function invocation or making GenServer calls, but this sample will step things up a bit by using GenStage[6] to accommodate multiple sources of injection, an event pipeline, and optional consumers that act as notifiers.

---

6.   https://hexdocs.pm/gen_stage/GenStage.html

The code for this sample might seem like it's got a bit more boilerplate than we'd like, but that's because you're deliberately using nothing but Elixir features like GenStage. In later chapters, you'll see frameworks, libraries, and products that can help remove some of the ceremony from the process.

To get started, use mix to create a new project with an empty supervision tree:

```
mix new flight_tracker --sup
```

Now let's create a stage that has a simple set of functions that will inject events into the stage. Naturally, this stage is a Producer.

notify_inject/flight_tracker/lib/flight_tracker/message_broadcaster.ex

```elixir
defmodule FlightTracker.MessageBroadcaster do
  use GenStage
  require Logger

  def start_link(_) do
    GenStage.start_link(__MODULE__, :ok, name: __MODULE__)
  end

  @doc """
  Injects a raw message that is not in cloud event format
  """
  def broadcast_message(message) do
    GenStage.call(__MODULE__, {:notify, message})
  end

  @doc """
  Injects a cloud event to be published to the stage pipeline
  """
  def broadcast_event(evt) do
    GenStage.call(__MODULE__, {:notify_evt, evt})
  end

  @impl true
  def init(:ok) do
    {:producer, :ok, dispatcher: GenStage.BroadcastDispatcher}
  end

  @impl true
  def handle_call({:notify, message}, _from, state) do
    {:reply, :ok, [to_event(message)], state}
  end

  @impl true
  def handle_call({:notify_evt, evt}, _from, state) do
    {:reply, :ok, [evt], state}
  end

  @impl true
  def handle_demand(_demand, state) do
    {:noreply, [], state}
  end
```

```elixir
  defp to_event(%{type: :aircraft_identified,
      message: %{icao_address: _icao, callsign: _callsign,
      emitter_category: _cat} = msg
    }) do
    new_cloudevent("aircraft_identified", msg)
  end

  defp to_event(%{type: :squawk_received,
    message: %{squawk: _squawk, icao_address: _icao} = msg}) do
    new_cloudevent("squawk_received", msg)
  end

  defp to_event(%{type: :position_reported, message: %{
    icao_address: icao, position: %{
      altitude: alt, longitude: long, latitude: lat}}}) do
    new_cloudevent("position_reported", %{
      altitude: alt, longitude: long, latitude: lat,
      icao_address: icao
    })
  end

  defp to_event(%{type: :velocity_reported, message:
    %{heading: _head, ground_speed: _gs, vertical_rate: _vr,
      vertical_rate_source: vrs} = msg}) do
    source =
      case vrs do
        :barometric_pressure -> "barometric"
        :geometric -> "geometric"
        _ -> "unknown"
      end

    new_cloudevent("velocity_reported", %{msg | vertical_rate_source: source})
  end

  defp to_event(msg) do
    Logger.error("Unknown message: #{inspect(msg)}")
    %{}
  end

  defp new_cloudevent(type, data) do
    %{
      "specversion" => "1.0",
      "type" => "org.book.flighttracker.#{String.downcase(type)}",
      "source" => "radio_aggregator",
      "id" => UUID.uuid4(),
      "datacontenttype" => "application/json",
      "time" => DateTime.utc_now() |> DateTime.to_iso8601(),
      "data" => data
    }
    |> Cloudevents.from_map!()
    |> Cloudevents.to_json()
  end
end
```

The broadcast_message function is to be called by whatever component wishes to perform an injection. The message (if necessary) is converted into a cloud event and then passed down to any interested stage consumers. You may notice that some unused fields are included in the pattern matching function heads. Other ways to match on these structures exist, but being explicit about the desired shape helps readability.

Let's create the code for the aircraft projector, which maintains a record for each flight for which it has received data.

notify_inject/flight_tracker/lib/flight_tracker/craft_projector.ex
```elixir
defmodule FlightTracker.CraftProjector do
  alias FlightTracker.MessageBroadcaster
  require Logger
  use GenStage

  def start_link(_) do
    GenStage.start_link(__MODULE__, :ok)
  end

  def init(:ok) do
    :ets.new(:aircraft_table, [:named_table, :set, :public])

    {:consumer, :ok, subscribe_to: [MessageBroadcaster]}
  end

  # GenStage callback for consumers
  def handle_events(events, _from, state) do
    for event <- events do
      handle_event(Cloudevents.from_json!(event))
    end

    {:noreply, [], state}
  end

  defp handle_event(%Cloudevents.Format.V_1_0.Event{
         type: "org.book.flighttracker.aircraft_identified",
         data: dt
       }) do
    old_state = get_state_by_icao(dt["icao_address"])

    :ets.insert(
      :aircraft_table,
      {dt["icao_address"], Map.put(old_state, :callsign, dt["callsign"])}
    )
  end

  defp handle_event(%Cloudevents.Format.V_1_0.Event{
         type: "org.book.flighttracker.velocity_reported",
         data: dt
       }) do
    old_state = get_state_by_icao(dt["icao_address"])

    new_state =
```

```elixir
      old_state
      |> Map.put(:heading, dt["heading"])
      |> Map.put(:ground_speed, dt["ground_speed"])
      |> Map.put(:vertical_rate, dt["vertical_rate"])

    :ets.insert(:aircraft_table, {dt["icao_address"], new_state})
  end

  defp handle_event(%Cloudevents.Format.V_1_0.Event{
        type: "org.book.flighttracker.position_reported",
        data: dt
      }) do
    old_state = get_state_by_icao(dt["icao_address"])

    # These coordinates are in CPR, not the familiar GPS format we're used to
    new_state =
      old_state
      |> Map.put(:longitude, dt["longitude"])
      |> Map.put(:latitude, dt["latitude"])
      |> Map.put(:altitude, dt["altitude"])

    :ets.insert(:aircraft_table, {dt["icao_address"], new_state})
  end

  defp handle_event(_e) do
    # ignore
  end

  def get_state_by_icao(icao) do
    case :ets.lookup(:aircraft_table, icao) do
      [{_icao, state}] ->
        state

      [] ->
        %{icao_address: icao}
    end
  end

  def aircraft_by_callsign(callsign) do
    :ets.select(:aircraft_table, [
      {
        {:"$1", :"$2"},
        [
          {:==, {:map_get, :callsign, :"$2"}, callsign}
        ],
        [:"$2"]
      }
    ])
    |> List.first()
  end
end
```

If you're not familiar with ETS or Registry select syntax, this code may seem befuddling:

```
:ets.select(:aircraft_table,
  [
    {
      {:"$1", :"$2"},
      [{:==, {:map_get, :callsign, :"$2"}, callsign}],
      [:"$2"]
    }
  ])
|> List.first()
```

This syntax comes straight from Erlang and is as powerful as it's confusing. The first term in the triple passed to :ets.select is the set of variables to pull from the table, indicated by their index preceded by a $ sign. The second is a predicate that indicates that all returned data must pass to be included in the results. The third and final term is a set of the columns to be returned. Some online tools can help you craft ETS selection syntax, so it's not as painful as it may first appear.

Written in something like SQL, the query might look like this:

```
SELECT craftdata FROM aircraft WHERE craftdata.callsign == callsign
```

While this isn't exactly pure (or even usable) SQL, hopefully, it makes the ETS select syntax a bit less mystifying. The select is pulling the entire map stored under the key whenever the map's callsign field equals the input variable.

The unique key of the aircraft projector's ETS table is something called an ICAO address, which is guaranteed to be unique per plane by the International Civil Aviation Organization ICAO. Since the plane's call sign (the human-friendly ID) can potentially arrive *after* receiving things like location, it needs to be okay that the aircraft projection has nothing but an ICAO address stored. This is one of those fun modeling situations where the right model can make things easy, and the wrong one can make things difficult or even impossible. You'd be surprised how often the "partial information event" pattern appears in real apps, where information is gathered from multiple sources (such as call signs, positions, and other identifiers) over time for the same entity.

An example of an ICAO address, encoded in hexadecimal, is AC82EC, which is the 24-bit address of the Shuttle Carrier Aircraft, the plane tasked with carrying the space shuttle.

Airplane positions are reported in CPR (Compact Position Record) format. The algorithm[7] to convert between CPR coordinates and the GPS coordinates most people recognize is outside the scope of this book.

Airplane Position Reports

Airplane positions are reported as Compact Position Records. This format is, as the name implies, an efficient and compact way to transmit coordinates. For the sake of brevity, the code samples leave these numbers as-is in CPR format. As a fun exercise, you might try adding a CPR decoder either as a producer-consumer stage or as a function in the aircraft projection.

Getting ADS-B Messages

If you've decided to play with some of the fun hardware and get an RTL-SDR dongle and an antenna, then you should be able to start pulling ADS-B messages "out of thin air" assuming you have clear access to the sky and are in an area where planes typically fly overhead.

If you don't want to fuss with the hardware, you can use the sample file included in this chapter's code samples that contains a number of demonstration ADS-B records that look something like this:

```
*5d4d20237a55a6;
*8d4d2023586db441dd891cb93e18;
*8d4d202399108fabe87c14860c91;
*8d4d202399108fabe87c14860c91;
*8d4d2023586d90aa979ce05a73c1;
*8d4d202399108fabe87814be3a91;
*8d4d202399108fabe87814be3a91;
```

These strings are called "Mode S"[8] encodings. When you're pulling the information from an RTL-SDR, you still need a process that pulls data from the dongle and makes it available to a user. The de facto standard for that is an application called dump1090.[9] You'll want to install this on your machine if you want to work with real data, though if you're a Mac user you may want to look for dump1090-mac because building dump1090 from source on a Mac is often difficult.

To keep things easy for you and to avoid spending more time setting up a flight monitor station than learning about event sourcing, the downloads for

---

7.   http://www.lll.lu/~edward/edward/adsb/DecodingADSBposition.html
8.   https://mode-s.org/decode/book-the_1090mhz_riddle-junzi_sun.pdf
9.   https://github.com/MalcolmRobb/dump1090

this chapter provide a version of this data already converted into JSON cloud events. If you were using dump1090 against a live data source, you would open a TCP socket to the network port, read the Mode S strings, decode them, and then finally convert them into JSON cloud events. Such a process could be built as a producer GenStage.

Now create the following GenServer, which can be started pointing to a sample data file. Each time a line is read from the file, it will invoke the MessageBroadcaster.broadcast_event/1 function, triggering the flow of data down the GenStage pipeline. A bit of a delay occurs before this code starts reading the file, which is a convenience to human developers running this inside iex. This provides a pretty good imitation of what it might look like to pull the data line-by-line from a TCP socket.

notify_inject/flight_tracker/lib/flight_tracker/file_injector.ex
```elixir
defmodule FlightTracker.FileInjector do
  alias FlightTracker.MessageBroadcaster
  use GenServer
  require Logger

  def start_link(file) do
    GenServer.start_link(__MODULE__, file, name: __MODULE__)
  end

  @impl true
  def init(file) do
    Process.send_after(self(), :read_file, 2_000)

    {:ok, file}
  end

  @impl true
  def handle_info(:read_file, file) do
    File.stream!(file)
    |> Enum.map(&String.trim/1)
    |> Enum.each(fn evt -> MessageBroadcaster.broadcast_event(evt) end)

    {:noreply, file}
  end
end
```

Next, build the flight notifier. This is an OTP process that's started for a specific flight call sign. So, if you want to explicitly monitor Pragmatic Programmer Airlines flight 250, you might start this process as follows:

```elixir
iex> GenServer.start_link(FlightTracker.FlightNotifier, "PRAG250")
```

Now create the code for the notifier, which simulates the external notification (which could be talking to a mobile device push notification service, for example) by emitting a log message.

notify_inject/flight_tracker/lib/flight_tracker/flight_notifier.ex
```elixir
defmodule FlightTracker.FlightNotifier do
  alias FlightTracker.MessageBroadcaster
  alias FlightTracker.CraftProjector

  require Logger
  use GenStage

  def start_link(flight_callsign) do
    GenStage.start_link(__MODULE__, flight_callsign)
  end

  def init(callsign) do
    {:consumer, callsign, subscribe_to: [MessageBroadcaster]}
  end

  # GenStage callback for consumers
  def handle_events(events, _from, state) do
    for event <- events do
      handle_event(Cloudevents.from_json!(event), state)
    end

    {:noreply, [], state}
  end

  defp handle_event(
         %Cloudevents.Format.V_1_0.Event{
           type: "org.book.flighttracker.position_reported",
           data: dt
         },
         callsign
       ) do
    aircraft = CraftProjector.get_state_by_icao(dt["icao_address"])
    # it's possible that we don't have the callsign yet
    if String.trim(Map.get(aircraft, :callsign, "")) == callsign do
      Logger.info(
      "#{aircraft.callsign}'s position: #{dt["latitude"]}, #{dt["longitude"]}")
    end
  end

  defp handle_event(_evt, _state) do
    # we're not interested in anything else
  end
end
```

Pattern Matching Events

You might notice that the code up to this point in the book sometimes pattern matches in the function head and other times extracts data inside the function. This is mostly a style preference, but has a practical purpose as well. If a pattern match in a function head fails to find data because of a missing or optional field, it can crash the code. If, instead, you manually extract data inside the function, the function runs and you can then easily match or branch on missing data.

An interesting and subtle rule displayed in this code is that notifiers *are* allowed to read from projections. *However*, notifiers cannot assume that they're always looking at the most recent version of a projection.

Whatever is available needs to be "good enough" for the notifier. In other words, if your notifier reads from a projection to produce a notification, then your system needs to be fine with the idea that a projection might potentially be out of date at read time. You can use tools and frameworks to help guarantee global consistency and ordering, but those concepts are discussed in Chapter 11, "Scaling Up and Out," on page 159.

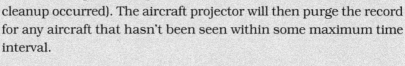

Writing a Cleanup Injector

As another fun exercise, write a cleanup injector and modify the aircraft projector. This injector will publish an event indicating that a cleanup interval passed (note that it doesn't indicate a cleanup occurred). The aircraft projector will then purge the record for any aircraft that hasn't been seen within some maximum time interval.

Remember, no looking at the real clock! To make this work, you'll need to compare the "last seen" stamp on the projection with the timestamp on the cleanup interval event, subtract, and then see if the interval has been exceeded. If you add this functionality to the flight tracker example, the projection should go away after a cleanup interval event occurs.

Running the Flight Tracker

To run the flight tracker, you need to set up the supervision tree and then run the application. Now create the application.ex file in the project's lib/flight_tracker directory:

```
notify_inject/flight_tracker/lib/flight_tracker/application.ex
defmodule FlightTracker.Application do
  use Application

  @impl true
  def start(_type, _args) do
    children = [
      {FlightTracker.FileInjector, ["./sample_cloudevents.json"]},
      {FlightTracker.MessageBroadcaster, []},
      {FlightTracker.CraftProjector, []},
      {FlightTracker.FlightNotifier, "AMC421"}
    ]

    opts = [strategy: :rest_for_one, name: FlightTracker.Supervisor]
    Supervisor.start_link(children, opts)
  end
end
```

The children automatically started are the following:

- The file injector (which starts injecting after a 2s delay to give humans a chance to see things start up)

- The message broadcaster (a GenStage producer)

- The craft projector (a GenStage consumer)

- A sample flight notifier preconfigured to a certain flight (another GenStage consumer)

Now make sure your mix.exs file looks as follows:

```
notify_inject/flight_tracker/mix.exs
defmodule FlightTracker.MixProject do
  use Mix.Project

  def project do
    [
      app: :flight_tracker,
      version: "0.1.0",
      elixir: "~> 1.17",
      start_permanent: Mix.env() == :prod,
      deps: deps()
    ]
  end

  # Run "mix help compile.app" to learn about applications.
  def application do
    [
      extra_applications: [:logger],
      mod: {FlightTracker.Application, []}
    ]
  end
```

```
# Run "mix help deps" to learn about dependencies.
defp deps do
  [
    {:gen_stage, "~> 1.2.1"},
    {:cloudevents, "~> 0.6.1"},
    {:uuid, "~> 1.1"}
  ]
end
end
```

If you run the application by running mix deps.get and then just iex -S mix, after a short delay, your console log should get messages from the notifier like this:

```
13:33:26.339 [info]  AMC421's position: 8430.0, 100636.0
13:33:26.339 [info]  AMC421's position: 21835.0, 105696.0
13:33:26.339 [info]  AMC421's position: 21761.0, 105731.0
```

And then, you can verify that the aircraft projector has also been doing its job:

```
iex(1)> FlightTracker.CraftProjector.aircraft_by_callsign("AMC421")
%{
  altitude: 20750,
  callsign: "AMC421",
  ground_speed: 376.78243058826405,
  heading: 157.85973327466598,
  icao_address: "4D2023",
  latitude: 21761.0,
  longitude: 105731.0,
  vertical_rate: -1792
}
```

If you feel like having even more fun with the samples, try adding more flights to the sample data file to see how the system behaves.

Wrapping Up

This chapter was important because it provided your first taste of trying to merge the purely functional world of event processing with the totally unpredictable real world using injectors and notifiers as event-sourced I/O. You applied that knowledge to building a real-time flight tracking system based on input from live data feeds. In addition to the fun of the sample, you learned foundational patterns and started to develop an instinct for when to inject and notify, so that when it comes time to build a large application, you'll be ready.

From an Elixir standpoint, you also played with GenStage as a technique for having multiple downstream consumers for a single producer.

In the next chapter, you'll learn how to create long-running, stateful processes that expand on the ideas of event-sourced I/O to build the final type of building block: the *process manager*.

## CHAPTER 4

Exploring the Saga of the Process Manager

Now that you've finished the first three chapters, your toolbox includes commands, events, aggregates, projectors, notifiers, and injectors. You've created purpose-built read models and encountered some laws of event-sourced applications. In this chapter, you'll explore the last of the fundamental building blocks of event-sourced systems: *process managers*. A process manager is responsible for managing stateful, long-running processes. Here, "long-running" means anything that requires multiple events and commands to complete. In other words, the length refers to the plurality of events that make up the process and *not* the passage of time. Other resources you encounter might refer to process managers as *sagas*, but for consistency throughout the rest of the book, the term *process manager* will be used.

Behaviorally, a process manager is the inverse of an aggregate: it consumes events and emits commands. Process managers are the choreographers who help event-sourced systems dance. They react to events that indicate the flow of a process and take appropriate action by issuing commands to aggregates.

Modeling a Process

A recurring theme throughout this book is that the model and design of an event-sourced system are often more important than the code itself. Modeling process managers may be the best example of this theme.

Writing a function that takes an event and returns a command is relatively easy, but figuring out when you should and should not be using a process manager often proves far more difficult.

The simplest possible process has a discrete beginning, middle, and end. In technical terms, that means an event must *start* the process, one or more events may *advance* the process, and one or more events must *stop* the process.

Required and Optional Events

 Pay special attention to the use of *may* and *must* here. A process always requires an inciting event and at least one terminating event. Advancing events, while common, isn't required.

Process managers have internal state in much the same way that aggregates do. Rather than being used for external consumption, the state is used to validate events and populate commands.

Activities and exercises such as Event Storming[1] are excellent for teasing out the flow of events through an application domain. Event Storming is a formalized, collaborative process for holding workshops and brainstorming sessions that can tease out event models and flows from subject matter experts. I've facilitated a number of these internally within companies, and the results have always been excellent and participants seem to enjoy the process.

But even after Event Storming and other exercises, determining how and when to use process managers can be confusing.

You can ask a few questions to help determine if you need a process manager for a given flow:

- Does this flow have a discrete beginning, middle, and end?

- Does this flow take action in response to events?

- Is the state of this flow meaningful beyond simple "started" and "completed" events?

- Is this flow potentially repeatable multiple times for a single entity?

If you answered yes to one or all of the above, you *probably* want a process manager. To help you decide, you can sketch out an illustration of your flow with a "boxes and arrows" diagram that shows these elements (you'll see an example of this in the next section):

- The inciting event (starts a flow)
- One or more advancing events (the "middle")
- The *commands* issued by the process manager in response to each event
- The completing events (the "end")

---

1. https://www.eventstorming.com/

Drawing such diagrams requires little initial investment of time and energy, and they can be invaluable in vetting potential processes. (You'll see many such diagrams throughout the rest of this chapter.)

A sequential description of the most basic flow might read like this:

1. Inciting event occurs
2. Process manager instantiates state, possibly emits command
3. Advancing event occurs
4. Process manager updates state, possibly emits command
5. Completing event occurs
6. Process manager finishes

Depending on whether you're modeling explicit failure, or how fine-grained your events are, process managers can sometimes emit commands as a sort of "last gasp" as the process halts. Make sure that these commands can't invalidate the completed status of the process.

The details behind the state management of a process manager are largely up to the implementer and whatever library or event sourcing toolset you're using. In some scenarios, a process manager's state is kept around indefinitely as a historical record, while in others the state is tossed once a success or failure has been determined (with projectors potentially storing only the important bits).

Implicit in this discussion is that it will be extremely rare for process managers to exist for flows of less than three events. When this does occur, the process has a starting event, one or more completing events, and no intermediate advancing events.

Creating a Simple Process Manager

The canonical "hello world" sample of process managers is usually a batch processor. You're going to build a process manager that advances the handling of a batch of files. The nature of these files or what needs to be done to them isn't relevant to this exercise.

The process starts when an initiating event, batch_created, is received. From there, the process manager issues a single command requesting work from an aggregate for each of the files in the batch. Thereafter, the process manager keeps tabs on the processing status of each of the files, as shown in the figure on page 50.

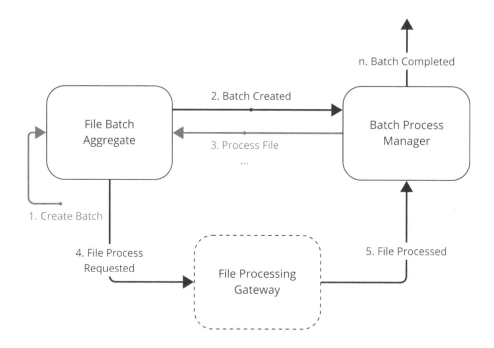

The flow through the system in an error-free path might be:

1. A batch is created via the create_batch command.

2. The file batch aggregate then emits the batch_created event.

3. *The process manager creates and dispatches one command per file on the batch.*

4. The file batch aggregate (not coded for this sample) emits a file processing requested event, which is picked up by a notifier/gateway.

5. When the file processing (external) is completed, the injector/gateway dispatches the file_processed event.

6. *The process manager updates its internal state upon receipt of file-processed events.*

While this might seem like a lot of busywork, you'll only be creating the process manager for this flow and assuming that the rest of the system has already been taken care of. Before creating the next bit of code, make sure to take note of the next law of event sourcing: "Work Is a Side Effect."

Work Is a Side Effect

A frequently asked question in new event sourcing projects is "where does the work happen?" Aggregates aren't allowed to perform side effects or read from external data. Process managers aren't allowed to perform side effects or read from external data. Projectors can create external data, but they can't perform "work" either.

If you follow the rule that work is a side effect, things may be easier to understand. If work is a mutation of the world outside the event-sourced system, then work is a side effect, and side effects are only allowed through gateways. The core primitives of aggregates, projectors, and process managers must never do work.

For this sample, create a GenServer that reacts to the batch_created and file_processed events. You can create an application to hold this GenServer by typing mix new batch --sup in your favorite shell. Add a process_manager.ex file to lib/batch:

chap4/batch/lib/batch/process_manager.ex
```elixir
defmodule Batch.ProcessManager do
  use GenServer

  def start_link(%{id: _id} = state) do
    GenServer.start_link(__MODULE__, state)
  end

  def init(%{id: id}) do
    {:ok,
     %{
       id: id,
       files: %{},
       status: :idle
     }}
  end

  def handle_call({:process_event, evt}, _from, state) do
    handle_event(state, evt)
  end

  defp handle_event(
         state,
         %{
           event_type: :batch_created,
           files: files
         }
       ) do
    f = Enum.map(files, fn f -> {f, :pending} end) |> Map.new()

    state = %{
      state
      | files: f,
        status: :created
```

```elixir
    }
    reply =
      Enum.map(files, fn f ->
        %{
          command_type: :process_file,
          file: f
        }
      end)

    {:reply, reply, state}
  end

  defp handle_event(state, %{
         event_type: :file_processed,
         file: %{id: file_id, status: file_status}
       }) do
    files = Map.put(state.files, file_id, file_status)

    state = %{
      state
      | files: files,
        status: determine_status(files)
    }

    # To add functionality we could send retry commands for those
    # files that have failed

    {:reply, [], state}
  end

  defp determine_status(file_map) do
    cond do
      Enum.all?(
        file_map,
        fn {_f, status} -> status == :success end
      ) ->
        :success

      Enum.any?(
        file_map,
        fn {_f, status} -> status == :error end
      ) ->
        :error

      true ->
        :pending
    end
  end
end
```

The code in this process manager implements the process flow outlined in the preceding diagram. The process manager GenServer is created by calling start_link. Note that in this example the starting or provisioning of an OTP process is done out of band from the event handling. This is to keep things simple for this example. How loosely or tightly coupled the lifetime of a process manager is to the lifetime of an OTP process (or another kind of process/thread) depends entirely on which frameworks and tools you're using. You'll encounter examples of multiple types of server lifetimes throughout the book.

The process manager begins its life with the status of :idle and, after receiving a batch-created event, quickly switches to :created. In response to this batch-created event, the process manager returns an array of commands: one for each file that needs to be processed.

It then listens for :file_processed events coming back from the file-processing gateway and continues to adjust its internal state accordingly. The biggest piece of business logic contained in this process manager is the determination of the status of the batch process. The process is considered successfully completed if all files were processed successfully, it's in error if one or more files failed processing, or otherwise the status is :pending.

Now use iex to interact with the sample process manager (line feeds in commands are for human-friendly output only and not part of the command):

```
$ iex -S mix
iex(1)> {:ok, pid} = Batch.ProcessManager.start_link(%{id: "batch1"})
{:ok, #PID<0.194.0>}
iex(2)> GenServer.call(pid,
  {:process_event, %{event_type: :batch_created, files: ["f1", "f2", "f3"]}})
[
  %{command_type: :process_file, file: "f1"},
  %{command_type: :process_file, file: "f2"},
  %{command_type: :process_file, file: "f3"}
]
iex(3)> GenServer.call(pid, {:process_event,
  %{event_type: :file_processed, file: %{id: "f1", status: :success}}})
[]
iex(4)> GenServer.call(pid, {:process_event,
  %{event_type: :file_processed, file: %{id: "f2", status: :success}}})
[]
iex(5)> GenServer.call(pid, {:process_event,
  %{event_type: :file_processed, file: %{id: "f3", status: :success}}})
[]
iex(6)> :sys.get_state(pid)
%{
  files: %{"f1" => :success, "f2" => :success, "f3" => :success},
  id: "batch1",
  status: :success
}
```

In the preceding iex session, you took on the role of a "meatspace aggregate" and manually converted the commands emitted by the process manager into events. In a complete system, the aggregate would automatically have processed those commands. Responding to each :file_processed event advances the overall state of the process manager. When all files have been processed, the manager's status moves to :success.

Depending on your application's needs, the completed process manager state might be marked for deletion or cleanup, or you might want to leave the state around for historical queries. If you want to periodically "sweep" your process manager state to clean it up, but you want summary data to remain, then you'll need to create a projector that emits the summary data. Another law of event sourcing has appeared: "All Projections Must Stem from Events."

All Projections Must Stem from Events

 Every piece of data produced by any projector *must* stem from at least one event. You cannot ever create projection data based on information from outside the event stream. Doing so would violate other event sourcing laws and ruin your system's ability to participate in replays.

This law also means never producing projections at timed intervals unless you're injecting stimulus events.

So far, so good. This should give you an idea of the kind of code that typically goes into a process manager. At this point, it would be easy to start adding more state and managing other semirelated activities within this one module, but that would violate the next law of event sourcing: "Never Manage More than One Flow per Process Manager."

Never Manage More than One Flow per Process Manager

 Each process manager is responsible for a single, isolated process. Its internal state represents an instance of that managed flow (for example, "Order 421," "Batch 73," or "New User Provisioning for User ABC"). As tempting as it may be to create a process manager for "orders" or "users," never lump multiple process flows into a single manager. Doing so generally means the failure of one flow can cascade out throughout the system. Keeping flows separate also avoids accidentally corrupting one process state with that of another.

Next, let's go through the process of modeling another sample domain where you'll build a slightly more complex process manager.

Building an Order Fulfillment Process Manager

The learning curve for event sourcing isn't linear. Some parts are easier to learn than others, and one area many people find challenging is process managers. They might be challenging, but they're crucial to real-world systems. Thankfully, the more domains you model with event sourcing, the easier it gets to design process managers.

In this section, you'll build a more realistic (and capable) process manager for *order fulfillment*. After a modeling exercise, your team might produce a diagram like the following that describes the flow of order fulfillment:

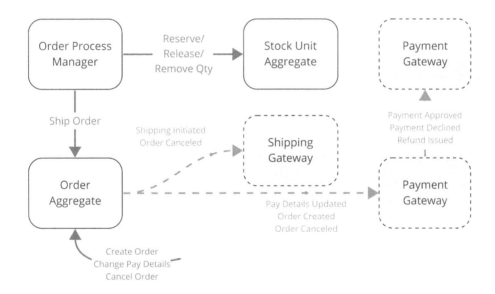

This diagram loosely describes a process where orders are created and managed, interact with an external payment system and with the external shipping/fulfillment system.

Diagrams like this might seem strange, but thankfully many techniques exist to make modeling and visualization of complex domains easier. You'll explore them in Chapter 11, "Modeling and Discovering Application Domains," on page 139. For now, let's try to tackle and reduce the complexity at hand.

The first step is to outline the responsibilities of a single entity within the system because trying to view the entire system as a whole is often impossible.

Let's derive a set of properties of the order fulfillment process manager from the diagram. In the list below, f(x) -> y simply means that a function applied to event x yields the command y.

- f(order_created) -> reserve_quantity
- f(order_canceled) -> release_quantity
- f(order_shipped) -> remove_quantity
- f(payment_approved) -> ship_order
- f(payment_declined) -> nil
- f(payment_details_updated) -> ship_order

To help focus on smaller parts of the diagram, categorize the events that the process manager needs in terms of their corresponding phase:

- *Start*—order_created
- *Advance*—payment_approved, payment_declined, payment_details_updated
- *Stop*—order_shipped, order_canceled

Other ancillary elements from the diagram are the gateways: *payment* and *shipping.* These are notifier/injector hybrids that manage outside interactions with an external payment system and the external shipping system. This is where the "work" is done.

It may seem overly simplistic to model an order fulfillment flow this way, but this feels like a good blend of realism and simplification "hand waving" to keep the example both meaningful and easily digested.

As with the earlier example of building a simple process manager, you'll only be coding the process manager here. If you want to code the aggregates, projectors, and gateways as a fun exercise, the first three chapters provide you with all the tools you need to do so.

First, create your empty stub project by typing mix new order_fulfillment --sup into your shell. Remember that process managers are fine-grained and built specific to a single process. So you don't have an all-encompassing "order process manager." Instead, you'll build one just for fulfillment in the module fulfillment_pm.ex. It might seem like there's a lot of code here but much of it is scaffolding:

chap4/order_fulfillment/lib/order_fulfillment/fulfillment_pm.ex
```
defmodule OrderFulfillment.ProcessManager do
  use GenServer

  def start_link(%{id: _id} = state) do
    GenServer.start_link(__MODULE__, state)
  end
```

```elixir
def init(%{id: id}) do
  {:ok, %{id: id, status: :created, items: []}}
end

def handle_call({:process_event, evt}, _from, state) do
  handle_event(state, evt)
end

defp handle_event(state,
  %{event_type: :order_created, items: order_items}) do

  cmds =
    Enum.map(order_items, fn item ->
      %{ command_type: :reserve_quantity, aggregate: :stock_unit,
        quantity: item.quantity, sku: item.sku} end)

  state = %{state | status: :created, items: order_items}

  {:reply, cmds, state}
end

defp handle_event(state,
  %{event_type: :payment_approved,order_id: oid}) do
  cmds = [
    %{ command_type: :ship_order, aggregate: :order,
      order_id: oid}]

  state = %{state | status: :shipping}
  {:reply, cmds, state}
end

defp handle_event(state,
  %{event_type: :payment_declined}) do
  state = %{state | status: :payment_failure}
  {:reply, [], state}
end

defp handle_event(_state,
  %{event_type: :order_canceled}) do
  {:stop, :normal, %{}}
end

defp handle_event(state,
  %{event_type: :order_shipped}) do
  cmds =
    Enum.map(state.items, fn item ->
      %{ command_type: :remove_quantity, aggregate: :stock_unit,
        quantity: item.quantity, sku: item.sku} end)

  {:stop, :normal, cmds, %{}}
end

defp handle_event(state,
  %{event_type: :payment_details_updated}) do

  cmds = [
    %{ command_type: :ship_order, aggregate: :order,
```

```
      order_id: state.id}]
    state = %{state | status: :shipping}
    {:reply, cmds, state}
  end
end
```

As with the earlier example of building a simple process manager, every event handler returns a list of commands (even if that list is empty). Pieces of the system you don't have to code in this chapter, like the gateways and aggregates, all move the gears of the machine forward.

In this iex session, you'll pretend to be those external gears (the return of the meatspace aggregate!) that move the process manager forward (as usual, line breaks are cosmetic):

```
iex(1)> {:ok, pid} =
  OrderFulfillment.ProcessManager.start_link(%{id: 12})
iex(2)> GenServer.call(pid,
  {:process_event,
    %{event_type: :order_created, items: [
      %{sku: "WIDGETONE", quantity: 5},
      %{sku: "SUPERITEM", quantity: 4}
    ]
  }})
[
  %{
    aggregate: :stock_unit,
    command_type: :reserve_quantity,
    quantity: 5,
    sku: "WIDGETONE"
  },
  %{
    aggregate: :stock_unit,
    command_type: :reserve_quantity,
    quantity: 4,
    sku: "SUPERITEM"
  }
]
```

Here you've simulated the creation of an order by passing the order_created event to the process manager. Note that although you don't do anything with the value returned from GenServer.call (a list of commands), the process manager has updated its internal state.

In the same session, create a simulated event from the payment gateway indicating that the payment for a given order was approved. In response to the payment approval, the process manager will issue the "ship order" command to the order aggregate.

```
iex(3)> GenServer.call(pid,
  {:process_event,
    %{
      event_type: :payment_approved,
      order_id: 12
    }
  })
[
  %{aggregate: :order,
    command_type: :ship_order,
    order_id: 12
  }
]
iex(4)> :sys.get_state(pid)
%{id: 12, status: :shipping, items: [ ... ]}
```

At this point, if you're thinking that process managers look a lot like state machines, then you'd win a prize. In fact, in many formal implementations of process managers, state machines do the majority of the heavy lifting internally. Conceptually, you can think of process managers as command-emitting state machines, where commands are emitted during a state transition.

Now simulate an error-free path where the order shipped without incident:

```
iex(3)> GenServer.call(pid,
  {:process_event,
    %{
      event_type: :order_shipped,
      order_id: 12
    }
  })
[
  %{
    aggregate: :stock_unit,
    command_type: :remove_quantity,
    quantity: 5,
    sku: "WIDGETONE"
  },
  %{
    aggregate: :stock_unit,
    command_type: :remove_quantity,
    quantity: 4,
    sku: "SUPERITEM"
  }
]
iex(4)> Process.alive?(pid)
false
```

Here the code shuts the GenServer down and also returns a set of commands to remove previously reserved stock quantity.

Building a User Provisioning Process Manager

Developing the muscle memory that supports modeling event-sourced systems is essential to being able to build event-sourced applications that grow and thrive in production and can be maintained by large teams.

As an exercise in developing that muscle memory, you're going to follow the same process you did earlier, but this time the code won't be provided for you. You can build as many or as few of the primitives as you like, but you should at least build the process manager.

The process that you're going to build is a pretty common one: the new user provisioning process. In the process described by the following diagram, two things need to happen when a new user is provisioned:

- Provision a user database—Each user in this application gets their own database, provisioned during the initial setup phase.

- Generate avatar—Each user gets an avatar that's dynamically generated from their metadata. This generation is done by an opaque activity on the other side of a gateway.

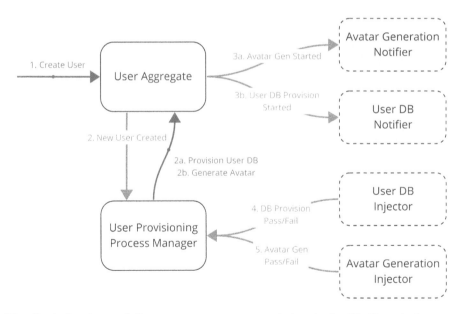

The first step in modeling a process manager is to start with the whole process view and then derive all of the small, actionable pieces as you did with order fulfillment.

In this diagram, instead of showing gateways, the injector and notifier halves have been drawn separately to show that a gateway can be a single monolithic process or a logical combination of many different components. Gateways can be software you write or even off-the-shelf products.

Another change from the previous flow is that failures are explicitly modeled now. In the order fulfillment process, error conditions were basically ignored. In this new user provisioning example, discrete events are emitted when things fail. This is a more mature and realistic flow that can be improved upon to support things like retries, backoffs, alerting, and more.

Note that there's a very subtle point about the definition of failure here. These failures indicate that some activity did fail. This is different than an aggregate rejecting a command because of validation failures. Aggregates rejecting commands *do not produce events* while process components that indicate true failure are represented as events.

In the paper, "Life Beyond Distributed Transactions: An Apostate's Opinion,"[2] Pat Helland says, "In a world where atomic transactions are not a possibility, tentative operations are used to negotiate a shared outcome." The further down the rabbit hole into distributed systems you go, the more you'll see how common it is to explicitly model error conditions and tentative operations.

For this exercise, write a process manager that choreographs new user provisioning. It should begin its flow when a user is created and complete its flow when each of the activities (DB provisioning and avatar generation) has completed, regardless of success. The status of the process should reflect the status of the individual activities.

The difference between choreography and orchestration will come up countless times in your exploration of event-sourced and distributed systems. If you take a look at the preceding diagram, you can get a good feel for the actions performed by each component.

User Aggregate

1. Accepts the CreateUser command

2. Emits the NewUserCreated event—an indication of a new, empty aggregate and *not* an indication of process completion

3. Accepts and validates the ProvisionUserDb and GenerateAvatar commands

4. Emits the AvatarGenerationStarted and DbProvisioningStarted events

---

2. https://www.ics.uci.edu/~cs223/papers/cidr07p15.pdf

User Provisioning Process Manager

1. Accepts the `DbProvisioningPassed` and `DbProvisioningFailed` events
2. Accepts the `AvatarGenerationPassed` and `AvatarGenerationFailed` events
3. When both database provisioning and avatar generation result events are received, emits either `UserProvisioningSucceeded` or `UserProvisioningFailed` events

Feel free to write as much or as little of the detail code as you like. Later on in the book, you'll see more examples with patterns similar to this exercise. You don't need to write the aggregate if you just want to simulate that component within an iex session so you can focus solely on the process manager.

Wrapping Up

With the conclusion of this chapter, you've now worked with all of the fundamental building blocks of event sourcing systems, culminating in an exploration of process managers, one of the more difficult primitives to learn to use properly. Event sourcing is similar to the board game Go in that the core set of rules is easy to learn and remember, but mastering the game itself can take a long time.

In the upcoming chapters, you'll take the toolbox you've developed so far and apply it to building applications that tackle real problems without any sleight of hand. You'll apply aggregates, projectors, process managers, gateways, commands, and events to create practical solutions and further remove fear and uncertainty from the realm of event-sourced applications.

## CHAPTER 5

Building Event-Sourced Elixir Apps with Commanded

So far, you've played with the basic building blocks of event-sourced applications: commands, events, aggregates, projectors, and process managers. You explored how to deal with the harsh reality of interacting with the outside world using injectors and notifiers. Up until now, you've been working with small, bite-sized pieces of code and relatively contrived samples.

Small samples are helpful for getting your feet wet with new concepts, but in this chapter, you're going to use all of the building blocks at your disposal to build a *real* application. You'll design, model, and implement an event-sourced application using the Elixir Commanded[1] library.

Commanded codifies a number of patterns and concepts that line up quite well with the opinions you've seen so far in this book. It supports defining event-sourced applications, dispatching events and commands, aggregates, and even process managers.

Deciding Where to Start

Looking ahead at the massive full scope of any project you want to build can be intimidating, even more so with something like event sourcing, where many people fear apocalyptic consequences if they get it wrong. The first thing you'll need is an idea of what you're going to build. I've taken care of coming up with this idea for you (you're welcome), which will be discussed in the next section. Once you have an idea, building the application is a matter of chopping the enormous scope into small, manageable pieces and repeating that until you're done.

---

1. https://hexdocs.pm/commanded/Commanded.html

Planning for an Iterative Process

To help you stay focused when working on tough projects, you can keep this analogy in mind. A properly laid out iterative plan starts with the first milestone of a unicycle, then a bicycle, a tricycle, a go-kart, and eventually a car. What you don't want to do is start by building a one-wheeled car. This analogy can help you focus on delivering complete features in an iterative timeline.

The upcoming chapters divide the seemingly unmanageable scope into meaningful chunks that you can work on one at a time.

Introducing Lunar Frontiers

Now that you understand our approach, let's start with the idea. In the not-so-distant future, humans have become a space-faring race and have reached out to the stars to find new, unexplored frontiers. These distant, moon frontiers are harsh and uninhabitable. Your mission, should you choose to accept it, is to be a lunar terraformer. You'll stake your claim on your own moon, and with nothing but your initial drop ship, a sense of humor, and courage, you'll prepare that moon for human colonization and habitation. The catch? Because the conditions on the surface are so harsh, all of the manual labor will be performed by robots: *robots that you must program.*

Players will write code, upload it into the various machines responsible for terraforming, and watch their new lunar frontier take shape. Note that "watch" here means looking at text. I lack any artistic ability so text adventures are the extent of my game creations. Further, the important part of this game is the event sourcing and not graphics.

Wish Fulfillment

I feel a need to fully disclose the motivation behind this example. Ever since I was 11 years old, I've been fascinated by the idea of user-generated content (UGC) games, especially those that teach. I've wanted to build a cooler version of CRobots (https://en.wikipedia.org/wiki/Crobots) ever since I first played with it. I've built various versions of the lunar frontiers idea in the past, but I've found that doing it as an event-sourced project is, without a doubt, the most fun. I hope you enjoy it as much as I do.

Embracing the Game Loop

One fascinating aspect of video game design is the concept of the *game loop.* Whether you're running a big-budget AAA title or an emulated copy of an old Atari 2600 game, underneath everything you can find what amounts to a simple while loop. During each iteration of this loop, the various elements of the game are given a chance to adjust their characteristics and ultimately render a *frame.* In a traditional game, a frame is a still image generated once per iteration of the loop. Like a classic animation flip book, if you flash frames fast enough, the human eye thinks their contents are moving. But our frames will be moments of state with no graphics.

On consoles and PCs, most game loops have fixed timing. You may see terms like "30 fps" or "60 fps." The "fps" here means *frames per second,* and that means exactly what you think it does—the number of still images the game engine will flash to the user every second. The more of them that are generated, the smoother the animation looks because your brain is extrapolating fewer "in-between" frames on your behalf. Although some game loops have fixed timing, others simply run as fast as they can, which can produce different experiences on different machines.

For the purposes of the Lunar Frontiers game, you'll also be using a game loop! If you think back on all of the laws of event sourcing, you probably already know how to build an event-sourced game loop. You'll be using an injector to drop "loop tick" events into the event stream. Each time one of these events arrives, the internal machinery will advance. What's really fun about combining event sourcing with game loops is that you can run the loop in real time (inject on system clock timed intervals), or you can run the loop as fast as the machine can go. This means the same event stream can be used to let people watch a game play out "live" if real time elapses between each tick event, or they can scroll through the game in "playback" mode if they missed it live.

Creating the First Flow

Within the Lunar Frontiers engine, the simplest possible flow is the creation of a new building. A player plants a construction site on a suitable piece of the lunar surface. (Technically, the player's robot, driven by code, does everything, but clarifying that all the time gets a bit tiresome, so the term player will be used throughout this text.) This construction site then advances its construction status on each tick of the game loop. When the construction is complete, the construction site "becomes" a usable building. The word *becomes* is in quotes because in most game engines (including this one) it's easier to delete the construction site and spawn[2] the appropriate building than to transform one unit type to another.

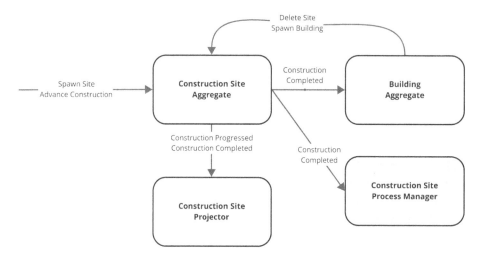

In this flow diagram, you can see two aggregates: Construction Site and Building. You could accomplish this kind of flow with a single building aggregate and have it manage internal state such as its "under construction" status, but that's an exercise for another chapter. In this flow, you have both a construction site and a building, so your construction progress can halt when you run out of resources and resume automatically when your coffers fill back up. This same pattern allows the construction site to be attacked and lose progress or be destroyed entirely. If we combine aggregates in this flow, we lose a lot of flexibility and potential enhancement avenues.

You'll break the problem down into tiny chunks of scope just as you did in the first four chapters of the book. First, create a new project that will hold your code for this chapter. You can use the provided scaffolding in the book's accompanying download in the lunar_frontiers_0 folder. This contains all the boilerplate and busywork to make things work properly without boring you with the details (yet). By convention, this chapter calls the target version lunar_frontiers_1, so on a Unix/Linux system you might do the following:

```
cp -R lunar_frontiers_0/ lunar_frontiers_1/
```

For the rest of the chapter, you'll be adding to and modifying the contents of the lunar_frontiers_1 folder.

---

2.   https://en.wikipedia.org/wiki/Spawning_(video_games)

Creating the Construction Site Aggregate

The flow diagram indicates that the construction site aggregate receives the following commands:

- f(spawn_site) -> site_spawned—This creates a new instance of this aggregate.
- f(advance_construction) -> construction_progressed, construction_completed—This command is dispatched during a game loop tick advance to move construction forward.

Having a construction site accept a discrete command to advance it allows the game engine to decide the rate at which sites advance based on game rules, and you don't have every site in the game build at the same rate.

The construction site aggregate handles the following events:

- site_spawned—A new construction site has appeared.
- construction_progressed—The site has made progress in building toward its goal.
- construction_completed—The site is finished and it can set its internal state to reflect this.

At this point, a lot of people get into a debate about which component determines when a thing like a construction site is completed. You saw this pattern in Chapter 4, "Exploring the Saga of the Process Manager," on page 47. Should the construction site aggregate emit construction_completed or should the process manager? This is a trick question because according to the laws of event sourcing, process managers *must never* emit events. This ends any philosophical debate and makes the choice clear. It's also fairly obvious that the aggregate is the authority of record with regard to its own completion status.

Now it's time to create this aggregate. Here you'll be introduced to some of Commanded's ceremony, but it should look *very* familiar if you've been reading the code samples so far. Since Commanded likes to have all of the event-sourced components in what it calls an "application," it makes a lot of sense to put the Commanded event-sourced application in its own module hierarchy so it can't be confused with your main OTP application.

Create a new file in lib/lunar_frontiers/app/aggregates/construction_site.ex:

```
lunar_frontiers_1/lib/lunar_frontiers/app/aggregates/construction_site.ex
defmodule LunarFrontiers.App.Aggregates.ConstructionSite do
  alias LunarFrontiers.App.Events.{
    SiteSpawned,
    ConstructionProgressed,
    ConstructionCompleted
  }
```

```elixir
alias LunarFrontiers.App.Commands.{SpawnSite, AdvanceConstruction}
alias __MODULE__

alias Commanded.Aggregate.Multi

defstruct [ :site_id, :site_type, :location, :required_ticks,
  :completed_ticks, :created_tick, :player_id, :completed,
  :completed_tick ]

# Command Handlers

def execute(
    %ConstructionSite{} = _site,
    %SpawnSite{site_id: id, site_type: typ,
    completion_ticks: ticks, location: loc, tick: now_tick,
    player_id: player_id }) do
  {:ok,
   %SiteSpawned{site_id: id, site_type: typ, location: loc,
     tick: now_tick, remaining_ticks: ticks, player_id: player_id}}
end

def execute(%ConstructionSite{} = site,
  %AdvanceConstruction{} = cmd) do
  site
  |> Multi.new()
  |> Multi.execute(&progress_construction(&1, cmd.tick, cmd.advance_ticks))
  |> Multi.execute(&check_completed(&1, cmd.tick))
end

defp progress_construction(site, tick, ticks) do
  {:ok,
   %ConstructionProgressed{site_id: site.site_id,
     site_type: site.site_type, location: site.location,
     progressed_ticks: ticks, required_ticks: site.required_ticks,
     tick: tick}}
end

defp check_completed(
    %ConstructionSite{
      completed_ticks: c, required_ticks: r} = site,tick
    )
    when c >= r do
  %ConstructionCompleted{
    site_id: site.site_id, player_id: site.player_id,
    site_type: site.site_type, location: site.location,
    tick: tick}
end

defp check_completed(%ConstructionSite{}, _tick), do: []

# State Mutators

def apply(%ConstructionSite{} = _site, %SiteSpawned{
    site_id: id, site_type: typ, location: loc,
    tick: now_tick, remaining_ticks: ticks, player_id: player_id
```

```
    }) do
  %ConstructionSite{
    site_type: typ, site_id: id,
    player_id: player_id, location: loc,
    created_tick: now_tick, required_ticks: ticks,
    completed_ticks: 0, completed: false}
end

def apply(
    %ConstructionSite{} = site,
    %ConstructionProgressed{} = event
  ) do
  %ConstructionProgressed{progressed_ticks: progressed} = event

  %ConstructionSite{
    site
    | completed_ticks: site.completed_ticks + progressed
  }
end

def apply(
    %ConstructionSite{} = site,
    %ConstructionCompleted{} = event
  ) do
  %ConstructionSite{
    site
    | completed: true,
      completed_tick: event.tick
  }
end
end
```

Don't worry about the fact that this file is using aliases for modules you haven't yet created. Remember you're building a unicycle, not a one-wheeled car, so you'll need the supporting types for this flow. You can see two familiar-looking functions in a Commanded aggregate's required callbacks:

- execute—This processes a command and returns one or more events. In the construction site code, you can see the use of Multi.new() to produce multiple events, including an optional construction_completed event via an elegant use of the pipeline operator.

- apply—This accepts an event and returns the appropriately modified state.

At this point, the motivation behind some of the choices in the first four chapters hopefully becomes a little clearer. For those new to Elixir, some of the syntax in this aggregate may look a bit verbose. This is because in Elixir pattern matching you can't use the "same name" shortcut that you can in other languages like TypeScript or Rust (for example, you can't destructure using %{bob} = data to extract the bob field; you have to be explicit: %{bob: bob} = data).

It also may look like we're doing little more than dumping fields from one struct to another. In the simplest case, that's what we're doing. But once we start building applications with real and complex business logic, developing the muscle memory for these patterns will come in handy.

Creating the Building Aggregate

As this chapter progresses, you'll spend a little less time analyzing the model and more time filling out the code as you should be exercising muscle memory at this point. The building aggregate represents a fully constructed unit in the game and is spawned in response to the completion of a construction site. (Hint: the process manager for construction sites will trigger this.)

Create a new file in lib/lunar_frontiers/app/aggregates/building.ex:

```
lunar_frontiers_1/lib/lunar_frontiers/app/aggregates/building.ex
defmodule LunarFrontiers.App.Aggregates.Building do
  alias LunarFrontiers.App.Events.BuildingSpawned
  alias LunarFrontiers.App.Commands.SpawnBuilding
  alias __MODULE__

  defstruct [:site_id, :site_type, :location, :player_id]

  def execute(%Building{} = _bldg, %SpawnBuilding{
        site_id: id, site_type: typ,
        location: loc, player_id: player_id
      }) do
    {:ok,
     %BuildingSpawned{
       site_id: id, site_type: typ, location: loc,
       player_id: player_id}}
  end

  def apply(%Building{} = _bldg, %BuildingSpawned{
        site_id: id, site_type: typ, location: loc,
        player_id: player_id}) do
    %Building{
      site_type: typ, site_id: id, player_id: player_id,
      location: loc}
  end
end
```

This is short and sweet. The building aggregate only does one thing at this point: *spawn*. It executes the spawn command and updates its own state upon receiving the spawned event. There's plenty of time for iterative enhancement in later chapters.

Creating the Game Loop Aggregate

This may be a slightly contested design choice. If you follow the idea behind an injector, then it's understood that you should be able to inject game loop advancement events. That's certainly true, and you could go that route. But this is another great opportunity to leave room for enhancement. For example, if any injector can dispatch advancement tick events, then there's nothing to control when the game's exit conditions have been met. If a game loop aggregate is responsible for validating the request for an advancement, it can then decide whether to issue an advanced event or a game completion event. Since the game doesn't currently have any exit conditions, the aggregate is nice and tiny:

lunar_frontiers_1/lib/lunar_frontiers/app/aggregates/gameloop.ex
```elixir
defmodule LunarFrontiers.App.Aggregates.Gameloop do
  alias LunarFrontiers.App.Aggregates.Gameloop
  alias LunarFrontiers.App.Events.GameloopAdvanced
  alias LunarFrontiers.App.Commands.AdvanceGameloop
  alias __MODULE__

  defstruct [:game_id, :tick]

  def execute(%Gameloop{} = _loop,
      %AdvanceGameloop{tick: tick, game_id: id}) do
    {:ok,
     %GameloopAdvanced{
       game_id: id,
       tick: tick
     }}
  end

  def apply(%Gameloop{} = _loop, %GameloopAdvanced{
    tick: tick, game_id: id}) do
    %Gameloop{
      game_id: id,
      tick: tick
    }
  end
end
```

Defining the Commands

In the interest of not bloating this chapter with extensive code listings, let's write out the properties of each command. The full code sample is available for you to use in the book's accompanying download. You can find the commands in lib/lunar_frontiers/app/commands/.

- advance_construction—requests the advancement of a construction site. Contains the number of ticks to advance (allowing sped-up enhancement from power-ups, and so on)

- advance_gameloop—requests the advancement of the game loop proper. The corresponding event will trigger multiple component executions.

- spawn_building—requests the creation of a building

- spawn_site—requests the creation of a construction site

Defining the Events

In the simplest of systems, the list of events should read like the past tense of the command names.

- building_spawned—indicates that a building has appeared on the game board (lunar surface)

- construction_completed—indicates a construction site has finished all necessary work

- construction_progressed—indicates construction progress has moved forward

- gameloop_advanced—many, many other pieces of code hang on this event like a finger pushing over a line of dominos

- site_spawned—indicates that a construction site has appeared

Managing the Construction Process

The code for the construction process manager is definitely worth examining. Create the file lib/lunar_frontiers/app/process_managers/construction.ex:

```
lunar_frontiers_1/lib/lunar_frontiers/app/process_managers/construction.ex
defmodule LunarFrontiers.App.ProcessManagers.Construction do
  alias LunarFrontiers.App.Events.{
    ConstructionCompleted,
    ConstructionProgressed,
    SiteSpawned,
    BuildingSpawned
  }

  alias LunarFrontiers.App.Commands.SpawnBuilding

  require Logger

  use Commanded.ProcessManagers.ProcessManager,
    application: LunarFrontiers.App.Application,
    name: __MODULE__
```

```elixir
@derive Jason.Encoder
defstruct [:site_id,:tick_started,:ticks_completed,
  :ticks_required,:status]

def interested?(%SiteSpawned{site_id: site_id}), do: {:start, site_id}
def interested?(%ConstructionProgressed{site_id: site_id}),
  do: {:continue, site_id}
def interested?(%ConstructionCompleted{site_id: site_id}),
  do: {:continue, site_id}
def interested?(%BuildingSpawned{site_id: site_id}),
  do: {:stop, site_id}
def interested?(_event), do: false

# Command Dispatch
def handle(%__MODULE__{},
      %ConstructionCompleted{site_type: site_type, site_id: site_id,
      location: location, player_id: player_id, tick: tick}) do
  %SpawnBuilding{
    site_id: site_id, site_type: site_type,
    location: location, player_id: player_id,
    tick: tick}
end

# By default skip any problematic events
def error(error, _command_or_event, _failure_context) do
  Logger.error(fn ->
    "#{__MODULE__} encountered an error: #{inspect(error)}"
  end)

  :skip
end
end
```

The first function worth exploring is interested?. This is a function that tells Commanded not only in which events the process manager is interested but also in which *phase* the event resides. Thinking back to Chapter 4, "Exploring the Saga of the Process Manager," on page 47, this is the same as defining which events *start*, *advance*, and *stop* a process. Here the corresponding keywords are :start, :continue, and :stop.

The handle function allows the process manager to convert an event into a command, while the error function can be used to deal with failure conditions. In the current implementation, the :skip atom will let the process manager stay up and running and ignore errors. Note that the code doesn't need to declare a handle function head for every interested event. The process manager will silently perform a no-op for unhandled (but interesting) events.

Routing Commands and Events

It's almost time to play the game! The last thing you'll need to do is set up routing and dispatching. Commanded needs to know which events and commands go to which aggregates, handlers, projectors, and so on. This is handled in the lib/lunar_frontiers/app/router.ex file:

lunar_frontiers_1/lib/lunar_frontiers/app/router.ex
```
defmodule LunarFrontiers.App.Router do
  alias LunarFrontiers.App.Commands.{
    AdvanceGameloop,
    AdvanceConstruction,
    SpawnSite,
    SpawnBuilding
  }

  alias LunarFrontiers.App.Aggregates.{
    Gameloop,
    ConstructionSite,
    Building
  }

  use Commanded.Commands.Router

  identify(Gameloop,
    by: :game_id,
    prefix: "game-"
  )

  identify(ConstructionSite,
    by: :site_id,
    prefix: "site-"
  )

  identify(Building,
    by: :site_id,
    prefix: "bldg-"
  )

  dispatch([AdvanceGameloop], to: Gameloop)
  dispatch([SpawnSite, AdvanceConstruction], to: ConstructionSite)
  dispatch([SpawnBuilding], to: Building)
end
```

The identify and dispatch macros are shortcuts for explicitly defining route rules for commands and events. When you look at the code supplied in the download, you'll find a file called systems_trigger.ex in the app/event_handlers folder.

lunar_frontiers_1/lib/lunar_frontiers/app/event_handlers/systems_trigger.ex

```elixir
defmodule LunarFrontiers.App.EventHandlers.SystemsTrigger do
  alias LunarFrontiers.App.Commands.AdvanceConstruction
  alias LunarFrontiers.App.Events.GameloopAdvanced
  alias LunarFrontiers.App.Application

  alias LunarFrontiers.App.Projectors.Building,
    as: BuildingProjector

  use Commanded.Event.Handler,
    application: Application,
    name: __MODULE__

  def handle(%GameloopAdvanced{tick: tick}, _metadata) do
    advance_construction(tick)
    :ok
  end

  defp advance_construction(tick) do
    for site_id <- BuildingProjector.active_sites() do
      %AdvanceConstruction{site_id: site_id,
        tick: tick, advance_ticks: 1
      }
      |> Application.dispatch()
    end
  end
end
```

Aggregate Identity

 It's more than passing coincidence that the field that uniquely identifies the aggregate is exactly the same as the field on the command sent to that aggregate. This is how Commanded can tell if a command is referring to a new or preexisting entity. While you can technically modify this behavior, it's generally a best practice to follow this convention, and fighting it will likely cause more trouble than it's worth.

This event handler might seem a bit confusing, and this is the first time you'll encounter a quirk of the library potentially influencing a modeling design. This function takes the single game loop tick and emits commands in a loop, emitting an advance_construction command for each active construction site.

An event handler that emits commands but *is not* a process manager is a specialized form of gateway that we will refer to as a *multiplexer*. This is done because Commanded process managers need the process key on every event they need. The gameloop_advanced event only contains two fields: :tick and :game_id.

In a perfect world, the construction process manager would be able to listen to each game loop tick and advance construction accordingly. When events are replayed, everything will remain consistent because both the game loop advance event and the construction advance events will be in the stream.

The silver lining here is that the systems_trigger.ex file gives you a central place where you can control advancement rates for various systems. This pattern is likely going to need to be repeated for multiple game flows, so this triggering multiplexer will get a lot of use. Without designing too far ahead, some possible candidates for this kind of pattern might include combat processes, trading, resource gathering and generation, and so on. This is also a prime example of where you're exchanging a little bit of purity for a large amount of practicality.

Playing the Game

Now, it's finally time to have some fun! To play the game, as you may have guessed, all you have to do is dispatch commands, and then the machinery takes over. To see the simplest possible loop (your unicycle), you'll submit the following commands:

- Advance game loop (tick 1)—This sets up the game and advances it to an initial position.

- Spawn site (required ticks 2)—This sets up a construction site that will take a total of 2 ticks to complete.

- Advance loop (tick 2)—Work progresses on the construction site.

- Advance loop (tick 3)—At this point, the construction site should magically become a building. You'll be able to confirm that in a number of ways.

This is what the iex session looks like (some lines have been removed for the sake of brevity, but note how much useful information you get from Commanded in debug mode):

```
$ iex -S mix
11:21:28.480 [info] Starting Lunar Frontiers Event Sourcing App
11:21:28.516 [debug] LunarFrontiers.App.EventHandlers.SystemsTrigger
  has successfully subscribed to event store
11:21:28.516 [debug] LunarFrontiers.App.Projectors.Building
  has successfully subscribed to event store
11:21:28.516 [debug] LunarFrontiers.App.ProcessManagers.Construction
  has successfully subscribed to event store
iex(1)> LunarFrontiers.App.Application.dispatch(
  %LunarFrontiers.App.Commands.AdvanceGameloop{game_id: 1, tick: 1})
```

```
11:21:58.907 [debug] Locating aggregate process for
`LunarFrontiers.App.Aggregates.Gameloop` with UUID "game-1"

11:21:58.912 [debug] LunarFrontiers.App.Aggregates.Gameloop<game-1@0>
 executing command: %LunarFrontiers.App.Commands.AdvanceGameloop{
  game_id: 1, tick: 1}

11:21:58.923 [debug] LunarFrontiers.App.ProcessManagers.Construction
 received 1 event(s)

11:21:58.933 [debug] LunarFrontiers.App.EventHandlers.SystemsTrigger
 received events: [%Commanded.EventStore.RecordedEvent{...}]

11:21:58.933 [debug] LunarFrontiers.App.Projectors.Building
 received events: [%Commanded.EventStore.RecordedEvent{...}]

11:21:58.934 [debug] LunarFrontiers.App.Aggregates.Gameloop<game-1@1>
  received events: [%Commanded.EventStore.RecordedEvent{...}]}]

11:21:58.934 [debug] LunarFrontiers.App.ProcessManagers.Construction
 is not interested in event 1 ("game-1"@1)
```

This makes it fairly obvious that all the wiring is properly connected and the gears are moving along happily. Next, spawn a construction site:

```
iex(3)> LunarFrontiers.App.Application.dispatch(
  %LunarFrontiers.App.Commands.SpawnSite{
    completion_ticks: 2, location: 1, player_id: 1,
    site_id: 1, site_type: 1, tick: 1
  })

11:22:39.197 [debug] Locating aggregate process for
`LunarFrontiers.App.Aggregates.ConstructionSite` with UUID "site-1"

11:22:39.198 [debug] LunarFrontiers.App.Aggregates.ConstructionSite<site-1@0>
  executing command: %LunarFrontiers.App.Commands.SpawnSite{
    site_id: 1, player_id: 1, site_type: 1,
    completion_ticks: 2, location: 1, tick: 1
  }
```

Note that Commanded has attempted to look up an aggregate with an ID of site-1. If it doesn't find a previously running one, it'll start a new one and manage its internal state.

Now we can advance the game loop twice more:

```
LunarFrontiers.App.Application.dispatch(
  %LunarFrontiers.App.Commands.AdvanceGameloop{
    game_id: 1, tick: 2})
...
LunarFrontiers.App.Application.dispatch(
  %LunarFrontiers.App.Commands.AdvanceGameloop{
    game_id: 1, tick: 3})
```

Skim through the debug logs (there will be a *lot* of them this time) and try to keep track of what's happening and where. You should see enough debug information to watch the construction site complete, the process manager issue a spawn building command, and the rest of the dominos all fall into place as expected. Now take a look at what the projector has stored:

```
iex(9)> :ets.tab2list(:buildings)
[
  {1,
   %{
     complete: 100.0,
     location: 1,
     player_id: 1,
     ready: true,
     site_id: 1,
     site_type: 1
   }}
]
iex(10)> :ets.tab2list(:sites)
[]
```

Congratulations! You've created your first event-sourced building on a lunar surface! You have plenty of room for refactoring, and you have no strong or specified data types (take a look at the location field, for example). In this first iteration, none of that matters. You can easily firm up some of that stuff as you add more features to the game in the subsequent chapters. For now, it's time to bask in the glory of your creation.

Before finishing up, you should take a look through the rest of the code not shown in this chapter. In particular, you should find the spot in the supervision hierarchy where the projector, explicit event handler, and process manager are all created. (Hint: they're all GenServers underneath the Commanded wrappers.) Also, take a look at the config/config.exs file, where you'll discover an important puzzle piece: the *event store*. This version uses an in-memory store, but Commanded supports multiple durable event stores that you'll see later. Also, make sure you find the line of code responsible for attaching the contents of router.ex to the application.

Wrapping Up

In this chapter, you took the skills and tools that you learned in the first four chapters of the book and applied them to building a real application: Lunar Frontiers. This application is a pure event-sourced application that plays a game by advancing a game loop, which in turn advances other processes and event flows that run the simulation of terraforming a hostile alien world.

You saw how to map the basic functions from the book's earlier chapters onto new primitives defined by the Commanded Elixir library. Throughout the upcoming chapters, you'll continue to iterate on the Lunar Frontiers game as you learn and apply new concepts and techniques. In the next chapter, you'll be applying the concept of replays and all that it entails.

## CHAPTER 6

Building Resilient Applications with Event Stores

While working your way through the book so far, your experience has been with ephemeral data. The functions you've written return data that vanishes into the ether, and the GenServers you've written lose their state once the OTP process stops. If you want data that will persist not only from chapter to chapter but also from disaster to schema evolution, you're going to need to choose, deploy, and utilize an event store.

In this chapter, you'll go through the process of learning how to decide on the right event store, persisting and replaying events, and making sure your event-sourced models are designed properly with replay and recovery in mind. Finally, you'll get to upgrade the Lunar Frontiers game from the previous chapter to run against a real, durable event store, bringing the game one step closer to a full production-grade application.

Evaluating Event and Projection Stores

The first step in choosing an event store needs to begin with understanding your requirements and that you're not limited to choosing a single product.

A key requirement is to define your application's data storage needs. An event-sourced system has three key types of persistent data, each with their own unique requirements:

- Aggregate state (snapshots)
- Projections (materialized views, read model)
- Event Log (write model)

Aggregate state, as you've seen, is a snapshot of data produced by applying a function to an event stream. The main interaction patterns for these snapshots are reading and writing by key in atomic operations. Aggregate state snapshots aren't obtained by querying a list of rows, so you want to optimize the snapshot store for fast reads from a single key. Key-value stores and NoSQL/document databases are often optimized in this fashion. Obtaining an aggregate's current state from a data store shouldn't require on-demand data operations like SQL joins or unions. You should be able to read or write an aggregate's state in constant time that doesn't get slower the bigger the system gets (called $O(1)$[1] time in some circles). A number of data storage products are available that have specialized support for snapshots.

Projections are a bit different. While they're also produced by applying functions to an event stream, their shape can vary greatly across different applications and domains. It's not uncommon for a projection to have rows (like the leader-board you created earlier in the book) as well as attached attributes. Projections can frequently be found both in relational databases as well as key-value stores, and even in graph databases. Applications can often have multiple projections for a single entity in a stream, each tailored to support a specific type of query in constant ($O(1)$) time.

The event log is the only source of truth within an event-sourced system. Everything else like projections and aggregate state can be destroyed and regenerated on demand so long as you still have the original event log. The so-called "live" or "online" event log is typically queried in time sequence, with little, if any, filtering done. These queries can start either at a specific event index number or a given time. For this reason, a *time series*[2] database is a popular choice for persisting the event log. In contrast to the "live" event log, many applications replicate the event data and then ship it off to different places to support more high-level analysis. *Complex event processing,*[3] data warehousing, and machine learning model training are all good examples of these offline event stores.

The important tip to take away from this section is that you should choose how you persist data *separately* for each of the three different data types in an event-sourced system. It's fairly common to use a smaller, easier-to-manage data store in development while the production environment uses multiple highly available data stores. If you can make your development

----

iterations easier and faster by choosing a single, easy-to-use data store during development and then use a more robust solution in production, it can make an enormous difference in developer experience (and happiness).

Replaying Events

The ability to replay events both for disaster recovery and upgrades and enhancements is one of the many underrated benefits of event sourcing. If you need to change a projection or aggregate, you can deploy the new code and simply replay events to generate the new state. If a piece of your application goes down and loses state, again replay is your new best friend.

You need to remember a few things when working with replays to keep your application safe, but as long as you're aware of those from the start, event replay will remain a beneficial tool in your arsenal. You've seen many of these things already as event sourcing laws, including never using wall clocks, never relying on information outside the event, limiting shared knowledge, and using referentially transparent functions, which is the most important thing for keeping replays consistent.

Verifying Models for Replay

Once you make the shift to a persistent event log after your initial experimentation period, you need to think about those events as being permanent, with no exceptions. Corrections come in the form of new events, not modification of old events.

This means that replays of historical events must never fail. Most importantly, if two successive replays of the same event log against fresh (empty) state can produce two different results, your event model is, in functional terms, "effectful." This means a side effect exists in the code and must be rooted out before you go live.

Thankfully, if you've been following all of the event sourcing laws up to this point, creating a replay-safe event log should be your default. When you get to Chapter 9, "Testing Event-Sourced Systems," on page 129, you'll get to do a lot of formal verification of your event model, and verification for replay will come along with that.

Capacity Planning

Very few applications have static consumption once running. To maintain an event-sourced application in production, you need to know your event log, state, and projection *growth rate*. Not only does the growth rate help you plan and configure your infrastructure, but it can also inform your application design. For example, a runaway growth rate might be a sign of an overly chatty (or worse, cyclic) event model that needs to be refactored.

To figure out a rough estimate of your growth rate, multiply the size of your biggest event by the number of events you expect to receive per hour, and then multiply that total by 720 (which is 30 days * 24 hours) to get a *very rough* estimate of your monthly storage requirements.

As an example, if your largest event consumes 2000 bytes and you expect to receive 1000 messages per hour, then you can plan on consuming 1440000000 bytes per month, or 1.34 gigabytes per month.

It might seem like a trivial exercise to calculate these numbers, but you should not only do this when starting but also update these results every month based on your measured usage. In this example, consuming 1GB/month is so cheap it doesn't rate anywhere near the top of the spending ranks for a typical application.

Keep Consumption in Perspective

 A good friend of mine is excellent at grounding me in reality and keeping my designs practical. By way of example, he once told me, "If you can fit your event log on an SD card, you don't have a capacity problem." These days, SD card capacity can be measured in terabytes. This serves as a great warning that it can be a large and costly mistake to overprepare for capacity you're not going to need.

Capacity planning for an event store and projections is an exercise that's basically the same as any other capacity planning activity. As such, the aspects of capacity planning that aren't specific to event sourcing are outside the scope of this book.

The biggest question you'll need to answer is how much of your event log is available in your live production environment. If you're using snapshots, then the "available" event log might be incredibly small, freeing you up to treat the offline portion of the event log with different I/O, storage, and performance requirements.

If you need to regenerate application state through a replay from the most recent snapshot, you should be in good shape if you plan on being able to hold the last several checkpoints/snapshots' worth of state and the event log.

The book goes into the scaling aspects of storing and managing event logs and state in Chapter 11, "Scaling Up and Out," on page 159.

Exploring Event Store

No discussion of persistent event stores would be complete without talking about *the* event store, *EventStoreDB*.[4] EventStoreDB is an open-source database that specializes in storing events (their documentation calls them "state transition events") and real-time streaming.

Storing and querying data in an EventStoreDB instance is a unique enough experience that it's worth going through a quick tutorial on it. It's easy to use, easy to install, and, with the right amount of effort, can support massive production installations.

To get started, you can either follow the instructions on the website to install the product on your machine or, more conveniently for this short exercise, run the following docker command to launch everything you need:

```
docker run --name esdb-node -it -p 2113:2113 -p 1113:1113 \
    eventstore/eventstore:latest --insecure --run-projections=All
```

Once you run this docker command and everything starts up cleanly, you should be able to open a browser window to http://localhost:2113 and bring up the administrative dashboard for the product. On Windows, the docker CLI syntax might be different. Consult the docker docs for your platform if the preceding command doesn't work.

The first thing you're going to do is add a couple of banking-related events to the account-ledger stream. Creating deposit and withdrawal events should be a comfortable habit for you by now.

---

4.   https://eventstore.com

An interesting thing about EventStoreDB (at least its Admin UI) is that to create a stream, you don't explicitly create it. Instead, the stream is created implicitly when you store an event on that stream.

Click Stream Browser and then the Add Event button. (You can find it in the top right corner.) I tried this on both Chrome and Safari, and in both cases, there's no blinking cursor showing you where the input is, so you need to manually click in the Stream ID field and type account-ledger.

For the event type, enter amountDeposited and a data payload consisting of the following JSON:

```
{
  "accountNumber": "ABC",
  "amount": 100
}
```

You can leave the metadata object empty and click the (also small and non-obvious) Add button in the bottom left corner of the window (you may need to scroll down).

Now you can click the "Stream Browser" button at the top, click in the account-ledger stream, and you should see something similar to the following screenshot:

Your timestamp (in the top right corner of the screenshot) and event ID (at the bottom) will be different than what's shown. Go ahead and add a couple more events for as many accounts as you like. The only requirements are that you use either amountDeposited or amountWithdrawn as the events and always use numbers in the amount field. Note that after you've created your first event, you now have an Add Event button at the top of the stream browser that pre-populates the stream name when looking at account-ledger.

This should all look pretty familiar. I urge you to explore, poke around, and read as much of the EventStoreDB documentation as you find interesting. It's a powerful tool, but it might not be the right tool for everyone.

Creating an EventStoreDB Projection

One area of the product that might be confusing, especially if this book is your first introduction to event sourcing, is EventStoreDB's use of projections. A projection in EventStoreDB is a combination of state produced by JavaScript code that runs against the stream and, optionally, emits events to output streams. A projection being able to emit roll-ups or other types of events to different streams can be an incredibly powerful tool, so long as your model and documentation have visibility into these streams.

To write a new projection, start by clicking Projections in the top navigation and then click the New Projection button. The name of the projection will be called account-balances, and it will run in Continuous mode. (Feel free to delve into the documentation on the difference between continuous and one-time projections.)

Enter the following code in the source field:

```
function getBalance(balances, accountNumber) {
    if (accountNumber in balances) {
        return balances[accountNumber];
    } else {
        return 0;
    }
}

options({
  $includeLinks: false,
  reorderEvents: false,
  processingLag: 0
})

fromStream('account-ledger')
.when({
  $init: function() {
    return {
      balances: {}
    }
  },
  amountDeposited: function(state, event) {
    const evt = JSON.parse(event.bodyRaw);
    const newbalance =
      getBalance(state.balances, evt.accountNumber) + evt.amount;
    state.balances[evt.accountNumber] = newbalance;
  },
```

```
  amountWithdrawn: function(state, event) {
    const evt = JSON.parse(event.bodyRaw);
    const newbalance =
      getBalance(state.balances, evt.accountNumber) - evt.amount;
    state.balances[evt.accountNumber] = newbalance;
  }
})
.outputState()
```

There's a lot going on here so let's go through it piece by piece. The options function call sets projection options. You can safely ignore those values for now.

The next important call is fromStream, which starts a fluent/builder-type syntax chain. The init function inside the when block is called when the projection is started without having processed any events (this includes a reset). Here, the code is creating an empty JavaScript object. I'm no JavaScript wizard, so I'm sure that far better ways exist for writing this code.

Next is a function called amountDeposited. This is the *exact, case-sensitive* name of the event type to be processed. In this case, it decodes the event, calculates the new balance, and then sets the balance in the mapping from account numbers to balances. This is the projection's state, which can be queried by anything that has sufficient privileges with the EventStoreDB client API (this includes the admin UI).

The amountWithdrawn function reduces the balance. Finally, the outputState() call stores the state of the projection. After saving the source, you'll want to hit the Reset button which will play all the old events through the projection. You should then see some JSON representing the new projection state in the Results panel:

```
{
  "balances": {
    "ABC": 95,
    "DEF": 100
  }
}
```

To produce this projection, the ABC account had a deposit of 100 and a withdrawal of 5, while the DEF account had a single deposit of 100.

One of the most difficult aspects of using EventStoreDB is figuring out which complexity you need and when you need it. It does a lot of powerful things, and that can be overwhelming when you're trying to explore the basic features.

Hopefully, when you're done working with EventStoreDB in this chapter, you'll be curious enough to peruse the EventStoreDB documentation and decide whether this database meets your needs for your own projects.

Upgrading Lunar Frontiers

The best way to experience the shift away from experimental mode, where everything is stored in memory and destroyed once the application stops, is to make these changes to a real application. In this section of the chapter, you'll take the Lunar Frontiers game from the previous chapter and upgrade it with a durable event log using Postgres. You'll also use this opportunity to clean up and refactor a few things.

First, copy the lunar_frontiers_1 application directory to a new one, lunar_frontiers_2. You'll be working out of this new directory for the next few sections of the chapter.

The Commanded library comes with a pluggable system for storing the event log. This means you can easily write an adapter for your favorite data store, but a number of off-the-shelf adapters are also readily available. You'll be working with the PostgreSQL adapter.

Confusing Names

In this section, you'll be working with the Commanded Event Store adapter. This adapter works with Postgres and *not* with the Event Store database software. This can get frustrating and confusing when reading documentation. For now, try to replace "Event Store Adapter" in your mind with "Postgres." Even more confusing is the fact that the adapter for EventStoreDB is actually called the Commanded *Extreme* Adapter, named after the HTTP client library that communicates with Event Store. Clear as mud.

To recap: to aid in memorizing, the *Event Store Adapter* is *PostgreSQL* while the *Extreme Adapter* is *EventStoreDB*.

Postgres is an easy-to-use database and is practically ubiquitous. The first thing you'll do is add a new dependency to your project (don't forget to run mix deps.get afterward) by editing the mix.exs file:

```
{:commanded_eventstore_adapter, "~> 1.4"},
```

With that in place, edit the config.exs file to contain the new configuration for the PostgreSQL Commanded adapter:

lunar_frontiers_2/config/config.exs
```
import Config

config :lunar_frontiers, LunarFrontiers.App.Application,
  event_store: [
    adapter: Commanded.EventStore.Adapters.EventStore,
    event_store: LunarFrontiers.EventStore
  ],
  pubsub: :local,
  registry: :local

config :lunar_frontiers, event_stores: [LunarFrontiers.EventStore]

config :lunar_frontiers, LunarFrontiers.EventStore,
  serializer: Commanded.Serialization.JsonSerializer,
  username: "postgres",
  password: "postgres",
  database: "eventstore",
  hostname: "localhost"
```

This configuration refers to a module, LunarFrontiers.EventStore, which you can add to the lib/lunar_frontiers directory as event_store.ex:

lunar_frontiers_2/lib/lunar_frontiers/event_store.ex
```
defmodule LunarFrontiers.EventStore do
  use EventStore, otp_app: :lunar_frontiers

  def init(config) do
    {:ok, config}
  end
end
```

This file is merely scaffolding at the moment, but it serves as an anchor location for a number of features and enhancements that are outside the scope of this book.

As you may have guessed, you're going to need to install PostgreSQL in your development environment (or run it as a Docker image, a virtual machine, and so on). For instructions on installing Postgres, take a look at the installation instructions.[5]

PostgreSQL on Linux

 It's been my experience that Postgres is hardest to install on Linux. While Windows and MacOS have nice installers, Linux can be confusing and error prone. If you run into problems with Linux, you can always use the stock Postgres docker image, set up a virtual machine, or even start a free instance of PostgreSQL in the cloud.

Now that you've got Postgres ready and the Lunar Frontiers project has the right configuration and dependencies, you can make use of a new mix plugin called event_store. This plugin has commands like create and init, which you can run in order as shown here:

```
> mix do event_store.create, event_store.init
==> gen_stage
...
Generated commanded app
==> lunar_frontiers
Compiling 21 files (.ex)
Generated lunar_frontiers app
The EventStore database has been created.
The EventStore schema already exists.
The EventStore database has been initialized.
```

The following screenshot taken on a Mac shows the Postgres environment and the newly created eventstore resources.

If you double-click the database, you'll be taken directly to a terminal session that's already logged in and has access to that database. This is a bit more finicky on Linux, so please take a look at the psql documentation to establish a similar session.

```
eventstore=# \dt public.*
             List of relations
 Schema |         Name         | Type  |  Owner
--------+----------------------+-------+----------
 public | events               | table | postgres
 public | schema_migrations    | table | postgres
 public | snapshots            | table | postgres
 public | stream_events        | table | postgres
 public | streams              | table | postgres
 public | subscriptions        | table | postgres
```

This looks promising! Run iex -S mix to bring up a REPL prompt with your supervision tree loaded and execute the dispatch function as shown:

```
iex(1)> LunarFrontiers.App.Application.dispatch(
...(1)>   %LunarFrontiers.App.Commands.AdvanceGameloop{game_id: 1, tick: 1})
```

You should see a bunch of text scroll across the terminal but there should be no errors. Taking a look at the Postgres database, we should see that the aggregate has successfully converted AdvanceGameloop into the GameloopAdvanced event:

```
eventstore=# select event_type, metadata from events;
                    event_type                     | metadata
---------------------------------------------------+--------------
 Elixir.LunarFrontiers.App.Events.GameloopAdvanced | \x7b7d
(1 row)
```

To exercise some projections and process managers, execute the following three additional dispatch functions for the SpawnSite and AdvanceGameloop (x2) commands.

```
iex(2)> LunarFrontiers.App.Application.dispatch(
  %LunarFrontiers.App.Commands.SpawnSite{
    completion_ticks: 2, location: 1, player_id: 1,
    site_id: 1, site_type: 1, tick: 1
  })
iex(3)> LunarFrontiers.App.Application.dispatch(
  %LunarFrontiers.App.Commands.AdvanceGameloop{
    game_id: 1, tick: 2})
iex(4)> LunarFrontiers.App.Application.dispatch(
  %LunarFrontiers.App.Commands.AdvanceGameloop{
    game_id: 1, tick: 3})
```

It should be no surprise to you that the projection is still using ETS tables to manage data.

```
:ets.tab2list(:buildings)
[
  {1,
   %{
     complete: 100.0,
     location: 1,
     player_id: 1,
     ready: true,
     site_id: 1,
     site_type: 1
   }}
]
```

But now you've got several more events, and, unlike in the previous chapter, these events aren't going away.

```
eventstore=# select event_type from events;
                        event_type
--------------------------------------------------------
 Elixir.LunarFrontiers.App.Events.GameloopAdvanced
 Elixir.LunarFrontiers.App.Events.SiteSpawned
 Elixir.LunarFrontiers.App.Events.GameloopAdvanced
 Elixir.LunarFrontiers.App.Events.ConstructionProgressed
 Elixir.LunarFrontiers.App.Events.GameloopAdvanced
 Elixir.LunarFrontiers.App.Events.ConstructionProgressed
 Elixir.LunarFrontiers.App.Events.ConstructionCompleted
 Elixir.LunarFrontiers.App.Events.BuildingSpawned
(8 rows)
```

Note that if you quit the application and start it back up again, the projection previously maintained in the in-memory ETS table will be *gone*. This is because all of the internal pointers in the database for Commanded event handler subscriptions indicate that all available events have been processed. In other words, the application thinks it's "caught up," so it doesn't need to reprocess any events. Since the ETS tables vanished as the process died, the projections are gone.

Now the need for persistent projections becomes more obvious.

We can force the projection to be regenerated by using the commanded.reset mix task. I found it difficult to execute mix commanded.reset from the terminal prompt and so opted for the more verbose (some might say *ugly*), yet more reliable, method of invoking the mix task from within iex:

```
iex(1)> Mix.Tasks.Commanded.Reset.run(["--app",
..(1)> "LunarFrontiers.App.Application", "--handler",
..(1)> "LunarFrontiers.App.Projectors.Building"])
Resetting "LunarFrontiers.App.Projectors.Building"
```

After a bunch of console output indicating that Commanded is reprocessing the event stream from the beginning, the building projector is reset. You can now verify that the in-memory read model projection has returned:

```
iex(2)> :ets.tab2list(:buildings)
[
  {1,
   %{
     complete: 100.0,
     location: 1,
     player_id: 1,
     ready: true,
     site_id: 1,
     site_type: 1
   }}
]
```

It should now be clear that managing in-memory projections isn't tenable in the presence of a durable event log. Nobody wants to have to manually reset projector subscriptions every time the application restarts, and that's certainly not going to work for an application running in production.

Adding Durable Projections to Lunar Frontiers

In the previous section, you converted the Lunar Frontiers application from being purely ephemeral to having a durable event store. In the process, you identified that the projection system needs to be similarly converted to a durable store. But before you go through the refactoring process on the projector, there's a bit of unfinished business in the application, and this is the ideal opportunity to take care of it.

Fixing a Weak Link

In all of the versions of the application so far, there's been a general-purpose event handler called SystemsTrigger that listens for game loop advancement (aka "ticks") and issues commands to move construction sites forward.

If you noticed something fishy about this event handler, then you've got a keen eye. This event handler ingests events and issues commands, *just as a process manager should*. The SystemsTrigger should be promoted to a real process manager, but that's not the biggest problem with this code. The systems trigger also violates another one of the event sourcing laws: "Process Managers Must Not Read from Projections."

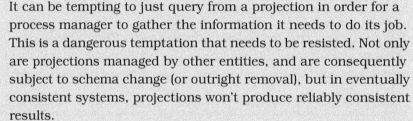

Process Managers Must Not Read from Projections

It can be tempting to just query from a projection in order for a process manager to gather the information it needs to do its job. This is a dangerous temptation that needs to be resisted. Not only are projections managed by other entities, and are consequently subject to schema change (or outright removal), but in eventually consistent systems, projections won't produce reliably consistent results.

This is one of the hardest of the laws to follow, and a lot of the arguments for violating it can sound reasonable. Done once, the consequences might seem insignificant, but this pattern permeated throughout an entire codebase can break consistency and, even worse, violate the predictable nature of replays.

You may remember that the game loop advance handler (systems trigger) queried the contents of a projection to figure out how many and what type of commands to send by examining the list of active construction sites. In the interest of keeping the samples small and easily digested, I hand-waved around this pattern as not being *too* bad, and this pattern sometimes helps people reason about their model state during prototyping. But this pattern should go no further than prototyping and should generally be avoided whenever possible.

With a bit of refactoring to the game flow, let's shore up this weak link in the code so that the foundation will be that much stronger to support future enhancements.

Now is a good time to grab the next iteration of the code by taking the contents of the lunar_frontiers_3 directory from the code downloads. A number of minor changes between revisions 2 and 3 could be easily missed, so it'll be easier to use version 3 and examine some of the specifics.

The first noteworthy change in the new code is the deletion of systems_trigger.ex from the event_handlers folder. You can also see a new game_loop_manager.ex file in the process_managers directory that contains the following code:

lunar_frontiers_3/lib/lunar_frontiers/app/process_managers/game_loop_manager.ex
```elixir
defmodule LunarFrontiers.App.ProcessManagers.GameLoopManager do
  require Logger
  alias LunarFrontiers.App.Commands.AdvanceConstruction

  alias LunarFrontiers.App.Events.{
    GameloopAdvanced,
    GameStarted,
    ConstructionCompleted,
    SiteSpawned,
    GameStopped
  }

  alias __MODULE__

  use Commanded.ProcessManagers.ProcessManager,
    application: LunarFrontiers.App.Application,
    name: __MODULE__

  @derive Jason.Encoder
  defstruct [
    :current_tick,
    :active_construction_sites,
    :game_id
  ]

  def interested?(%GameStarted{game_id: gid}), do: {:start, gid}
  def interested?(%SiteSpawned{game_id: gid}), do: {:continue, gid}
```

```elixir
def interested?(%ConstructionCompleted{game_id: gid}), do: {:continue, gid}
def interested?(%GameloopAdvanced{game_id: gid}), do: {:continue, gid}
def interested?(%GameStopped{game_id: gid}), do: {:stop, gid}
def interested?(_event), do: false

def handle(%__MODULE__{} = state, %GameloopAdvanced{tick: tick}) do
  sites = state.active_construction_sites || []

  construction_cmds = sites
    |> Enum.map(fn site_id ->
      %AdvanceConstruction{
        site_id: site_id,
        tick: tick,
        game_id: state.game_id,
        advance_ticks: 1
      }
    end)

  construction_cmds
end

def apply(%GameLoopManager{} = state, %GameloopAdvanced{tick: tick}) do
  %GameLoopManager{
    state
    | current_tick: tick
  }
end

def apply(%GameLoopManager{} = _state,
  %GameStarted{game_id: gid} = _evt) do
  %GameLoopManager{
    current_tick: 0,
    game_id: gid,
    active_construction_sites: []
  }
end

def apply(%GameLoopManager{} = state,
  %SiteSpawned{site_id: sid, tick: t} = _evt) do
  %GameLoopManager{
    current_tick: t,
    game_id: state.game_id,
    active_construction_sites: state.active_construction_sites ++ [sid]
  }
end

def apply(%GameLoopManager{} = state,
  %ConstructionCompleted{site_id: sid, tick: t} = _evt) do
  %GameLoopManager{
    current_tick: t,
    game_id: state.game_id,
    active_construction_sites: state.active_construction_sites -- [sid]
  }
end
```

```
  # By default skip any problematic events
  def error(error, _command_or_event, _failure_context) do
    Logger.error(fn ->
      "#{__MODULE__} encountered an error: #{inspect(error)}"
    end)

    :skip
  end
end
```

The most important thing to notice here is that the list of active construction sites is now being monitored by the *internal state* of this process manager. As you'll see shortly, the code is no longer using a projection for this data, and you can verify this by checking the projectors directory and seeing only the new building.ex module.

The game loop process manager is initialized by a new event, GameStarted (which needs to come from an aggregate). The only field on this event is game_id, as in the new GameStopped event. Both of these events can be found in the lib/lunar_frontiers/app/events directory.

While these events may seem sparse right now, it's super easy to enhance them later as the game progresses. To produce the GameStarted event, you'll need an aggregate that can emit it. This is easily added to the GameLoop aggregate:

```
def execute(%Gameloop{} = _loop, %StartGame{game_id: gid}) do
  event = %GameStarted{game_id: gid}

  {:ok, event}
end
```

You need to make a few more tiny tweaks and the refactoring is done. With the introduction of new events and commands, the router needs to be modified. Adding StartGame to the Gameloop dispatch as shown here sets up the beginning of that flow:

```
lunar_frontiers_3/lib/lunar_frontiers/app/router.ex
defmodule LunarFrontiers.App.Router do
  alias LunarFrontiers.App.Commands.{
    AdvanceGameloop,
    StartGame,
    AdvanceConstruction,
    SpawnSite,
    SpawnBuilding
  }

  alias LunarFrontiers.App.Aggregates.{
    Gameloop,
    ConstructionSite,
    Building
  }
```

```
use Commanded.Commands.Router

identify(Gameloop,
  by: :game_id,
  prefix: "game-"
)

identify(ConstructionSite,
  by: :site_id,
  prefix: "site-"
)

identify(Building,
  by: :site_id,
  prefix: "bldg-"
)

dispatch([AdvanceGameloop, StartGame], to: Gameloop)
dispatch([SpawnSite, AdvanceConstruction], to: ConstructionSite)
dispatch([SpawnBuilding], to: Building)
end
```

Almost done! In converting the systems trigger from a generic event handler to the new GameLoopManager, the application's supervision tree needs to be modified to start the right OTP GenServer. This is done by adding App.ProcessManagers.GameLoopManager to the list of modules to load in the supervisor.ex file.

```
def init(_arg) do
  children = [
    App.Application,

    App.ProcessManagers.Construction,
    App.ProcessManagers.GameLoopManager,

    App.Projectors.Building
  ]

  Supervisor.init(children, strategy: :one_for_one)
end
```

Finally, the game_id field is added to the commands and events that correspond to the ones declared by the process manager.

With V3 of Lunar Frontiers fresh from the oven, purge the event log using the following commands. The first will remove all of the event store schema from the database, and the second command, which you've seen once already, creates it all from scratch.

```
$ mix event_store.drop
$ mix do event_store.create, event_store.init
```

You might get an error that looks something like this:

```
** (Mix) The EventStore database couldn't be dropped, reason given:
"ERROR 55006 (object_in_use) database \"eventstore\" is being accessed by
other users.
There are 2 other sessions using the database."
```

You can easily get this error on a Mac with a terminal session open in this database. Simply close that session and retry, and the error should go away. The book's companion code has a script in the lunar_frontiers_3/scripts directory called reinit_store.sh that contains the preceding mix commands.

Projecting with Redis

It's time to take care of that ephemeral projection. In the real world, we need our projections to be durable because we'll need to be querying the generated read models, and those queries likely come from an entirely different part of the application than the writes. When I look for a place to store data, one of my primary criteria used to evaluate them is whether they're easy to run locally in my development loop but also easy (and potentially cheap) to run in a production environment. Redis is one of those data stores. It's very easy to get running (especially on Macs) locally, and a number of cloud providers either offer Redis databases or they offer a Redis-compliant interface on top of their own data store (Amazon's RDS does this).

While Redis is easy to install locally,[6] if you don't want a full install, you can run its docker image. Either is sufficient to go through this sample.

The first step is to add the redix library to mix.exs (which is already done in the lunar_frontiers_3 code). Next, take a look at the application.ex module, and you'll see a new process in the supervision tree:

```
{Redix, name: :projections}
```

This starts a Redis client using the default (anonymous, local, and default port) options and names the Redis connection :projections. Now you can take a look at the rewritten building projector that writes to Redis and no longer needs to maintain separate site data.

lunar_frontiers_3/lib/lunar_frontiers/app/projectors/building.ex
```
defmodule LunarFrontiers.App.Projectors.Building do
  alias LunarFrontiers.App.Events.BuildingSpawned
  alias LunarFrontiers.App.Events.SiteSpawned
  alias LunarFrontiers.App.Events.ConstructionProgressed
```

---

6. https://redis.io/docs/getting-started/installation/

```elixir
use Commanded.Event.Handler,
  application: LunarFrontiers.App.Application,
  name: __MODULE__

def init(config) do
  {:ok, config}
end

def handle(
      %SiteSpawned{
        site_id: site_id,
        site_type: site_type,
        location: location,
        player_id: player_id
      },
      _metadata
    ) do

  building = %{
    complete: 0.0,
    site_id: site_id,
    site_type: site_type,
    player_id: player_id,
    location: location,
    ready: false
  } |> Jason.encode!()

  Redix.command(:projections,
    ["SET", projection_key(site_id), building])
  Redix.command(:projections,
    ["SADD", player_sites_key(player_id), site_id])

  :ok
end

def handle(
      %BuildingSpawned{
        site_id: site_id,
        site_type: site_type,
        location: location,
        player_id: player_id,
        tick: t
      },
      _metadata
    ) do

  building = %{
    complete: 100.0,
    site_id: site_id,
    spawned_tick: t,
    site_type: site_type,
    location: location,
    player_id: player_id,
```

```elixir
      ready: true
    } |> Jason.encode!()

    Redix.command(:projections, ["SET", projection_key(site_id), building])

    :ok
  end

  def handle(
        %ConstructionProgressed{
          site_id: site_id,
          site_type: site_type,
          location: loc,
          player_id: player_id,
          progressed_ticks: p,
          required_ticks: r
        },
        _metadata
      ) do
    building = %{
      player_id: player_id,
      complete: Float.round(r / p * 100, 1),
      site_id: site_id,
      site_type: site_type,
      location: loc,
      ready: false
    } |> Jason.encode!()

    Redix.command(:projections, ["SET", projection_key(site_id), building])

    :ok
  end

  defp projection_key(id) do
    "building:#{id}"
  end

  defp player_sites_key(player_id) do
    "sites:#{player_id}"
  end
end
```

At this point, you've got a clean slate. You've got a process manager built the right way, and your projector is no longer ephemeral.

You *could* do things the hard way and start up the application via iex -S mix and then manually execute a set of commands to advance the event flow, but you can make it easier on yourself by using an Elixir script. This script provides a bit of foreshadowing of what you'll be doing in Chapter 9, "Testing Event-Sourced Systems," on page 129.

```
lunar_frontiers_3/scripts/single_site.exs
# from the parent directory, execute via:
# iex -S mix run scripts/single_site.exs

alias LunarFrontiers.App.Commands
import LunarFrontiers.App.Application

player_id = "px42"

gid = UUID.uuid4()
sid = UUID.uuid4()

IO.puts "New game #{gid}, going to build site #{sid}"

dispatch(%Commands.StartGame{game_id: gid})
dispatch(%Commands.AdvanceGameloop{game_id: gid, tick: 1})

dispatch(%Commands.SpawnSite{
  completion_ticks: 5,
  location: 1,
  player_id: player_id,
  site_id: sid,
  site_type: 1,
  tick: 1,
  game_id: gid
})

dispatch(%Commands.AdvanceGameloop{game_id: gid, tick: 2})
dispatch(%Commands.AdvanceGameloop{game_id: gid, tick: 3})
dispatch(%Commands.AdvanceGameloop{game_id: gid, tick: 4})
dispatch(%Commands.AdvanceGameloop{game_id: gid, tick: 5})
dispatch(%Commands.AdvanceGameloop{game_id: gid, tick: 6})
```

You can execute this script from the project's root directory with the following command:

```
iex -S mix run scripts/single_site.exs
```

This will start up your project and its full supervision tree, execute the contents of the single_site.exs script, and then leave you in an interactive iex prompt so you can poke around and make sure everything is working properly. Assuming Postgres and Redis are working fine, you shouldn't see any error messages.

At this point, you can use the psql session to check that the PostgreSQL event store has a stream for a uniquely identified game and site (your UUIDs will vary):

```
eventstore=# select stream_uuid from streams;
                 stream_uuid
-------------------------------------------
 game-b078a1a2-9f60-4f63-bc46-18380fdd82e2
 site-118eb988-c444-4085-925c-f870be657d7b
 $all
 bldg-118eb988-c444-4085-925c-f870be657d7b
(4 rows)
```

That's it! You've got a process manager that no longer relies on projections to make decisions and advance processes. The weak link is gone, and the foundation has been refactored to no longer violate any event sourcing law. To top it all off, you've got a durable projection for buildings sitting snugly in Redis.

To take a look at the projection stored in Redis, you can use a combination of the redis CLI and the command-line JSON parsing utility jq (the UUID for your projection will be different):

```
$ redis-cli GET building:118eb988-c444-4085-925c-f870be657d7b | jq
{
  "complete": 100,
  "location": 1,
  "player_id": "px42",
  "ready": true,
  "site_id": "118eb988-c444-4085-925c-f870be657d7b",
  "site_type": 1,
  "spawned_tick": 6
}
```

To get a feel for more long-running activity, feel free to copy the single_site.exs script and create your own flow. See what it's like to start multiple buildings in a row and watch them build and complete over "time."

Projecting with Ecto

The Commanded library also has a readily available plugin for building projectors that use Ecto. This plugin makes projector syntax easy to read and formalizes some patterns that are recommendations in other more bespoke projectors.

The following example illustrates the small and easy code you can use for projecting via Ecto:

```
defmodule Projector do
  use Commanded.Projections.Ecto,
    application: MyApp.Application,
    name: "my-projection",
    repo: MyApp.Repo,
    schema_prefix: "my-prefix",
    timeout: :infinity

  project %Event{}, _metadata, fn multi ->
    Ecto.Multi.insert(multi, :my_projection, %MyProjection{...})
  end

  project %AnotherEvent{}, fn multi ->
    Ecto.Multi.insert(multi, :my_projection, %MyProjection{...})
  end
end
```

This kind of projector still needs to be started in your supervision tree, but everything else is taken care of for you. This is an event sourcing book and not a book on either Elixir or Ecto. As such, an in-depth discussion of how to get Ecto set up, build repositories, set up configuration, and more is outside the scope of this book. *Programming Ecto*[7] is an excellent resource if you're interested in using Ecto in your applications.

Wrapping Up

Once your event stream goes from in-memory and ephemeral to a real, durable, replayable stream, then a whole bunch of code and patterns escape the "hello world" bubble. In this chapter, you went through the process of seeing what is involved in making it real from evaluating and comparing event and projection stores and capacity planning to upgrading the code for Lunar Frontiers to use a Postgres event log and Redis projections.

In the next chapter, you'll apply everything you've learned so far to the notion of evolutionary architectures and explore how event-sourced systems can safely change over time.

---

7. https://pragprog.com/titles/wmecto/programming-ecto/

## CHAPTER 7

Evolving Event-Sourced Systems

In the previous chapter, you learned about the importance of event stores and how they relate to additional storage for things like projections and aggregates. With those strong fundamentals in place, you can start exploring how event-sourced systems change over time and how to plan and build for this as a feature, and not something to fear.

In a blissful alternate universe, we could deploy our applications once, and they would continue to run unmodified and self-sustaining until the end of time. The unfortunate truth is that the moment we deploy our code anywhere, it's already *legacy*. Even if we never add a single feature, applications still need to change because of bug fixes, patches that deal with security vulnerabilities, or even simple version bumps of transitive dependencies.

This chapter provides a cookbook-like set of patterns for dealing with the paradox of immutable events in the face of ever-changing applications. Whether you're changing events or the code for the fundamental building blocks, all of those changes need to somehow work within the constraints of immutable events and all the other event sourcing laws.

Evolving Event Schemas

The evolution of events is often one of the most difficult and misunderstood aspects of maintaining event-sourced systems, so let's start there. The most important thing to remember for this section and throughout the rest of this chapter is another law of event sourcing: "Event Schemas Are Immutable."

Event Schemas Are Immutable

 Event schemas must never change. Any change to an event schema produces a brand-new event type. This means that each new version of an event is a unique type.

This law may seem a bit inflexible, so let's explore the reasoning behind it with some examples. Imagine that you've created an application that has an AccountCreated event. On this event, the fields are UserID, Name, Address, and Email. You deploy the first version of your application with this event, and, after some period of time, your application is successful and you end up with over 5,000 AccountCreated events.

After some change to your company's financial structure and profit model, you decide that you need a SubscriptionPlan field on the AccountCreated event. This is to handle a new feature where customers can pick a plan when they sign up.

Your application continues running, and, after a few thousand more account creation events, you decide that you also need the ServiceRegion field to accommodate your new location-based service and billing structure.

The evolution of your event might look like this:

AccountCreated	AccountCreated2	AccountCreated3
UserID Name Address Email	UserID Name Address Email **SubscriptionPlan**	UserID Name Address Email **SubscriptionPlan** **ServiceRegion**

At first glance, it looks like these data structures can all be backward compatible with each other. Using clever serialization techniques and optional or nullable fields, depending on how the data is stored, you could treat an AccountCreated event as though it were an AccountCreated3 event. *This path only leads to despair.*

Avoid the Backward Compatibility Trap

 Reject every evolution plan that includes the notion that a new version of an event is backward compatible with an old version. Just because you *can* add optional fields to a data structure doesn't mean you *should*. This violates the most recent law, which exists for a good reason.

Assume you did intend for AccountCreated2 to be backward compatible with all preexisting AccountCreated events. If the SubscriptionPlan field is missing from an event, you can fill it in with a reasonable default, right?

The problem with this is that *the default values are an assumption that comes from outside the event stream*. In other words, your code may assume that the absence of SubscriptionPlan implies a default value of free_trial, but what happens when that code changes? If the code processing those events changes, and the assumed default value when that field is missing also changes, then you've corrupted your application state by injecting external context (the presumed default value) that isn't stored in an event.

If AccountCreated and AccountCreated2 are never conflated, then you always have the option of managing and evolving the logic specific to each event schema version. But isn't this still relying on assumptions that come from outside the event stream?

This is a subtle but important point. With the "optional field" strategy, the assumption applies to the data in the event, which should be immutable. With the explicit versioning strategy, the assumption applies to the logic generating projections and aggregate state. The first assumption violates an unbreakable law while the second is standard procedure in event sourcing.

Despite their evolutionary nature, the existence of AccountCreated and AccountCreated2 in the event store represents the completion of two fundamentally different activities.

Missing data is a classic computer science problem. Is the presence of a null the explicit declaration of missing data, a bug that failed to generate required data, or worse, a data (de)serialization problem?

If you follow the backward compatibility strategy and treat all account creation events as some variant of AccountCreated3, can you ever really know the difference between an event that was missing a field because it predated the use of that field, a new event that intentionally left that field blank, or a new event that left it blank because of a bug?

You might think that you won't run into these kinds of edge cases, but if you plan on banning these situations outright, your event stream will continue to be the reliable source of truth it needs to be.

Evolving event schemas impacts your aggregates, projectors, and process managers. If you load all account creation events into the code by coercing everything into an AccountCreated3 event, you lose historical context.

That isn't to say that you can't reuse code to process the events. It only means that you should never do anything that obscures the difference between multiple event versions, so it's easier to follow the law and treat all event versions as distinct event types.

The advice from this section about evolving events can be distilled into the following items:

- A change to an event schema produces a new event schema.

- Events that are no longer used aren't deleted; they just stop occurring.

- Avoid the backward compatibility trap by not making assumptions about optional fields.

- We cannot change the past to accommodate new schemas or events.

Evolving Aggregates

Aggregates can change over time without breaking any of the rules. As your application and your understanding of how customers use it changes, you'll no doubt make changes to the internal workings of an aggregate.

These changes typically come in two forms:

- Change how it computes internal state
- Change the events emitted in response to commands

As with all evolutions, the timeline must be preserved. So, even though your aggregate may have changed in one or both of these ways, you cannot go back in time and reapply the new logic to old events. The following diagram shows time moving to the right. Note that the new aggregate has no power whatsoever over what happened before it was deployed.

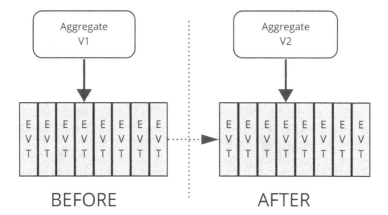

Remember that a replay only replays events. Commands are ephemeral and don't truly exist. They're simply one possible stimulus that produces an event. Once an event has been produced, your application owns it until the end of time.

An aggregate's internal state can change by replaying events that predate the newly deployed aggregate, but that doesn't alter the timeline, so it's allowed.

You'll explore evolving aggregates more closely and see some example code later in the "Evolving Lunar Frontiers" section of this chapter.

Evolving Projections and Projectors

Projections are disposable. They're the output of a function applied to an event stream and are never used by aggregates or process managers to make decisions. The reason why projections are disposable is that the data in a projection is *not* used by business logic and is *only* used as a consumer-facing read model. In other words, nothing on the *inside* of the perimeter of your event-sourced system relies on a given projection.

Let's say you have a user-profile projector, and it produces the user profile projection based on user-related events. Every time a UserProfileChanged event occurs, this projection changes. With version 1 of the projector, it stores the user's first name and surname combined in a single name field.

You then release version 2 of the projector, and, instead of combining those two values, you decide to keep them separate in the first-name and surname fields. To make this change, you'll need to deploy version 2 to replay the event stream through the projector.

Here's the most important question: *do versions 1 and 2 of the projection exist at the same time?* Unfortunately, the answer to that is a classic computer science refrain: *it depends.*

If you still have deployed code that expects the name field, then you can't safely remove that field. You can have the new projection exist under a different (preferably versioned) namespace, but then you end up with a stagnating projection and, over time, it's easy for developers to lose sight of *why* it wasn't updated.

A couple of common patterns are used when evolving projections:

- The new projector writes to a different projection, and old and new never overlap.

- The old projection is deleted, and the new projector generates the new projection in its place, breaking compatibility and forcing old code to update.

- The new projector adds the new field to the old projection alongside the old field, allowing both old and new consumers to co-exist.

The way in which a projector evolves is entirely determined by the needs of the code consuming the projection. The third pattern is likely to be the most potentially dangerous, as it's always hard to predict whether code actually is backward compatible, and the perils of the backward compatibility trap were already laid out earlier in the chapter.

Projectors cannot rely on *other* projections to compute projections. This is subtle but important. A projector can update the data it previously created (atomic updates are covered later in the book), but it cannot read from data managed by a different projector.

If you have a bank account projector and a customer projector, neither of them can read from the other's projections. If they need data that's common to both, then that data needs to come from the events used by each projector, and *not* from other projections.

This can be more concisely stated as another event sourcing law: "Different Projectors Cannot Share Projections."

Different Projectors Cannot Share Projections

 Projectors must share nothing with other projectors. They're free to update their own data but can neither read nor write projections managed by other projectors.

Evolving Process Managers

It should be second nature by now to remember that process managers take in events and emit commands that move a process forward. Since commands are ephemeral, the only evidence you have of a process's completion (or lack thereof) is the events that correspond to that process. Unprocessed or rejected commands leave no evidence behind (except maybe in logging/tracing, but that's another topic).

Process managers rarely evolve in isolation. If a process manager adds a new step to a process, that typically produces a new command which means an aggregate needs to be updated to handle that command. This in turn might produce a new event that the aggregate needs to handle to update internal state, and a projector might also be interested in this new event.

This means that no matter what change you make to a specific process manager, you cannot change how that process took place *in the past*. If you add steps to a process, those steps will only apply to new events.

Phrased another way, this means that evolving a process manager can be done by creating a new version of that process manager, ensuring that all other changes as a result adhere to the patterns in this chapter and don't violate any of the event sourcing laws.

Evolving Lunar Frontiers

To experience the evolution of an event-sourced system first hand, you'll be evolving the Lunar Frontiers game. It would be overwhelming and difficult to follow if you evolved aggregates, projections, and process managers all at the same time, so this section will focus only on the evolution of aggregates.

In the case of Lunar Frontiers, there's no need to have both a site and a building aggregate when we can just put a construction progress field on the building.

The current construction process starts with SiteSpawned, progresses via ConstructionProgressed, and then when it finishes with ConstructionCompleted, it issues a command to spawn a building, ultimately resulting in BuildingSpawned:

SiteSpawned -> ConstructionAdvanced -> ConstructionCompleted -> (command) -> BuildingSpawned.

The new process skips the concept of the site entirely:

BuildingSpawned -> ConstructionProgressed -> ConstructionCompleted

That should be it. The building aggregate should update its internal construction progress and eventually reach 100%. These events already exist in the log, so this process should be compatible and not alter the timeline. This also means that the game doesn't need to maintain the site's projection.

Question Everything

Don't assume that your first refactor design is the best. Question it iteratively until you've got something you're ready to build out as a prototype.

It would be pretty easy to go and get started on this refactor, but take another look at the new and improved flow. In this flow, there's still a Construction process manager that dispatches AdvanceConstruction commands.

But what if you dispatch the AdvanceConstruction command to a building aggregate instead of a process manager? The building aggregate could then emit ConstructionAdvanced (and potentially ConstructionCompleted). With the building being the only thing interested in those events, the Construction process manager becomes totally unnecessary.

So the new, *even more improved* plan is to remove the Site aggregate, remove the Construction process manager, create new versions of the commands and events when appropriate, and then test it all out.

It may be easiest to start by looking at the new game loop process manager, which is responsible for issuing the new advance construction command.

lunar_frontiers_4/lib/lunar_frontiers/app/process_managers/game_loop_manager.ex
```elixir
defmodule LunarFrontiers.App.ProcessManagers.GameLoopManager do
  require Logger
  alias LunarFrontiers.App.Commands.AdvanceConstruction

  alias LunarFrontiers.App.Events.{
    GameloopAdvanced,
    GameStarted,
    BuildingSpawned.V2,
    ConstructionCompleted,
    SiteSpawned,
    GameStopped
  }

  alias __MODULE__

  use Commanded.ProcessManagers.ProcessManager,
    application: LunarFrontiers.App.Application,
    name: __MODULE__

  @derive Jason.Encoder
  defstruct [
    :current_tick,
    :buildings_under_construction,
    :game_id
  ]

  def interested?(%GameStarted{game_id: gid}),
    do: {:start, gid}

  def interested?(%BuldingSpawned.V2{game_id: gid}),
    do: {:continue, gid}

  def interested?(%ConstructionCompleted{game_id: gid}),
    do: {:continue, gid}

  def interested?(%GameloopAdvanced{game_id: gid}), do: {:continue, gid}
  def interested?(%GameStopped{game_id: gid}), do: {:stop, gid}
  def interested?(_event), do: false

  def handle(%__MODULE__{} = state, %GameloopAdvanced{tick: tick}) do
    buildings = state.buildings_under_construction || []
```

```
    construction_cmds =
      buildings
      |> Enum.map(fn site_id ->
        %AdvanceConstruction{
          site_id: site_id,
          tick: tick,
          game_id: state.game_id,
          advance_ticks: 1
        }
      end)

    construction_cmds
  end

  def apply(%GameLoopManager{} = state, %GameloopAdvanced{tick: tick}) do
    %GameLoopManager{
      state
      | current_tick: tick
    }
  end

  def apply(%GameLoopManager{} = _state, %GameStarted{game_id: gid} = _evt) do
    %GameLoopManager{
      current_tick: 0,
      game_id: gid,
      buildings_under_construction: []
    }
  end

  def apply(
        %GameLoopManager{} = state,
        %BuildingSpawned.V2{site_id: sid, tick: t} = _evt
      ) do
    %GameLoopManager{
      current_tick: t,
      game_id: state.game_id,
      buildings_under_construction: state.buildings_under_construction ++ [sid]
    }
  end

  def apply(
        %GameLoopManager{} = state,
        %ConstructionCompleted{site_id: sid, tick: t} = _evt
      ) do
    %GameLoopManager{
      current_tick: t,
      game_id: state.game_id,
      buildings_under_construction: state.buldings_under_construction -- [sid]
    }
  end

  # By default skip any problematic events
  def error(error, _command_or_event, _failure_context) do
```

```elixir
    Logger.error(fn ->
      "#{__MODULE__} encountered an error: #{inspect(error)}"
    end)

    :skip
  end
end
```

The important change here is that this new game loop manager is maintaining a list of buildings under construction as part of its internal state. This means that process managers don't need access to projections, making them more testable and predictable in isolation. When a building is spawned, the game loop manager starts managing construction. When construction is completed, the process manager removes the building from the buildings_under_construction field.

Now let's take a look at the simplified router.ex file:

```elixir
lunar_frontiers_4/lib/lunar_frontiers/app/router.ex
defmodule LunarFrontiers.App.Router do
  alias LunarFrontiers.App.Commands.{
    AdvanceGameloop,
    StartGame,
    AdvanceConstruction,
    SpawnSite,
    SpawnBuilding
  }

  alias LunarFrontiers.App.Aggregates.{
    Gameloop,
    Building
  }

  use Commanded.Commands.Router

  identify(Gameloop,
    by: :game_id,
    prefix: "game-"
  )

  identify(Building,
    by: :site_id,
    prefix: "bldg-"
  )

  dispatch([AdvanceGameloop, StartGame], to: Gameloop)
  dispatch([SpawnBuilding.V2, AdvanceConstruction], to: Building)
end
```

Next, let's look at V2 of the building spawned event, which gives the rest of the simplified system the information it needs to advance and complete construction.

lunar_frontiers_4/lib/lunar_frontiers/app/events/building_spawned_v2.ex
```elixir
defmodule LunarFrontiers.App.Events.BuildingSpawned.V2 do
  # In this version of the event, a building is spawned with a
  # tick count indicating how many ticks until construction is completed
  @derive Jason.Encoder
  defstruct [:site_id, :game_id, :site_type, :location, :player_id,
             :tick, :completion_ticks]
end
```

The last thing that needed to change in this refactor was the supervision tree. Now that the app has fewer process managers, it has fewer supervisors to start:

lunar_frontiers_4/lib/lunar_frontiers/app/supervisor.ex
```elixir
defmodule LunarFrontiers.App.Supervisor do
  use Supervisor

  alias LunarFrontiers.App

  def start_link(arg) do
    Supervisor.start_link(__MODULE__, arg, name: __MODULE__)
  end

  @impl true
  def init(_arg) do
    children = [
      # Application
      App.Application,

      # Process Managers
      App.ProcessManagers.GameLoopManager,

      # Projectors (read model)
      App.Projectors.Building
    ]

    Supervisor.init(children, strategy: :one_for_one)
  end
end
```

Next, we'll examine an aspect of application evolution that's surprisingly controversial.

Migrating Event Streams

By now, a part of your brain should be permanently etched with the phrase, "the event log is immutable." Events are the sole source of truth, and they cannot be changed. This chapter has made it pretty clear that, if you need to evolve events and commands, you do so by *creating new ones* because a new version of an event is actually a brand-new event.

A number of frameworks will let you migrate from V1 of an event to V2 "in-place" as the stream is being processed. This doesn't break the rules so long as the meaning conveyed by the event doesn't change.

Here lies the controversy. I contend that if you can migrate an event to a new version in-memory during processing, then you should also be able to migrate that event *to a new stream.* In other words, as long as the upgrade doesn't change the meaning of the event, you can run your entire event stream through a migration process and *produce a new stream.*

A competing viewpoint is that you shouldn't create a new stream with the migrated events, as that violates event immutability. Instead, this strategy relies on event processors to upgrade the events as they're processed. My issue with this view is that you can violate event immutability by changing event processors and the way they upgrade events.

You should make up your own mind after playing with both options and examining your stream for the safety of upgrades.

Stream migration doesn't break the immutability law because the original remains intact and provides a large pile of advantages. My favorite advantage is that it gives you the ability to run "what if" scenarios against a separate event stream. Being able to move around in your application on a hypothetical stream can be invaluable.

A common practice is to run the migration, produce a new stream, and then run test suites against the new stream. All of this can be done without affecting production in any way. It's far easier to spot problems early this way than to use framework-specific features to upgrade events in-memory during processing. Note that the Commanded library supports in-place, in-memory event migration. I personally don't like this because it opens the door for bugs if you change (intentionally or otherwise) the code for the migrator.

An argument that will continue until the end of time is whether producing an "upgraded" stream violates immutability. It all comes down to how you've modeled the old and new events. In the Lunar Frontiers game, old events indicating building spawns didn't contain the ticks required for completion. This doesn't matter all that much because all of those old buildings have already completed their construction. If we want to be sticklers for detail, when we upgrade the events, we can always add the value for required ticks to the V2 events. Making an event more explicit is a common way to upgrade without changing its meaning.

Wrapping Up

Many books on evolutionary architectures are available, and entire courses are taught in computer science curriculums on how to evolve applications safely and reliably. Event sourcing is no exception. If you've been following all of the other event sourcing laws as you build your application, then migrating events, projections, and processes to new versions _should_ be straightforward. If you find it to be too difficult, then use that as a sign that something else might be amiss, like a potentially broken law or a way to model your way out of a corner.

Evolving event streams is a topic filled with conflicting opinions. If you model your system so that you're prepared to continually make changes to event schemas, projections, and more, then you should be in good shape to carry your application into the future.

In the next chapter, you'll dive into the topic of security and see how it applies to the various layers and components in event-sourced systems.

## CHAPTER 8

Securing Event-Sourced Applications

In the previous chapter, you learned some techniques to handle the evolution of event-sourced systems while still embracing the immutability of the event log. In this chapter, you'll learn how to secure event streams and the applications that rely on them.

Securing event-sourced applications can be tricky, especially if you're attempting to secure one that's already deployed and has built up a historical event stream. As you'll see throughout this chapter, security in event-sourced applications can be divided into the following zones:

- Aggregates and incoming command requests
- The event stream
- Sensitive information on events
- Projections
- Process manager state

Securing Event Streams

Before you secure any individual components, you should spend some time designing and establishing your security posture. Determine which individual pieces of your application need their own isolated security and which areas of your application are covered under a broader umbrella provided by other components. This section and the rest of this chapter will give you some useful rules and guides to help you establish this stance.

The event stream is the sole source of truth. If someone can tamper with, or add to, that source of truth, then any number of terrible things can happen. If an intruder can add an event to the stream, they can alter someone's account balance, steal funds and secrets, or wreak miscellaneous havoc. If an intruder can modify or delete existing events, then the consequences can be even more disastrous. Ultimately, this means that your security posture should never rely on inherited or assumed security. The event log is worth securing independently of every other aspect of an application.

When building on your laptop or even experimenting in development and staging environments, you can simply write messages to a broker's stream, publish, or otherwise add to the append-only event log. This is fine because you're running on your own machine, and you trust yourself, but this practice should be limited to the development iteration loop and extend no further.

When running anywhere else, you should never trust or assume that someone submitting an event to the log has the right to do so. It's easy to assume that things are secure when your event log is inside your organization and only visible to certain network addresses or segments. But that assumption can destroy an application if an intruder does manage to gain access.

The best security strategies stem from the phrase *trust no one* and the concept of *defense-in-depth*.[1] The way in which you secure access to your event stream depends almost entirely on what product or technology you're using to support that stream.

One of my favorite security mechanisms is *decentralized*, which means that some or all of your cloud assets can be compromised and you still have no loss of secrets. You can find an example of this in the NATS[2] message broker, which comes with a technology called JetStream that's ideal for event sourcing. With NATS, you can require that anyone attempting to write to your event log must present a JSON Web Token (JWT)[3] as well as a signed nonce proving that they're in possession of the right private key.

Not only does this require client credentials to write to the event log, but it also supports maintaining an audit trail that correlates events to the user that created them. This also means that code clients like an aggregate might also need credentials to emit events in response to commands.

Kafka, RabbitMQ, EventStoreDB, NATS, and countless other data stores all have their own specific authentication and authorization schemes. Whichever one you're using, you'll want to ensure that you routinely test to make sure that the event log cannot be accessed by those without the right permissions.

You might also want to lock down which entities can *read* the event log as well. You don't want this to be quarriable by arbitrary entities. Instead, you

---

1. https://csrc.nist.gov/glossary/term/defense_in_depth
2. https://docs.nats.io/nats-concepts/jetstream
3. https://jwt.io

want it to only be readable by aggregates, projectors, and whatever other clients are the core parts of your platform.

Cloud events are introduced first in Chapter 3, "Enforcing Perimeters with Injectors and Notifiers," on page 27. You might already be thinking about an opportunity to add layers of security to your event stream by leveraging the flexibility of the cloud event envelope.

For reference, here's a cloud event that you've already seen:

```
{
    "specversion": "1.0",
    "id": "2a0562bb-6657-4918-ad21-bec63f38bc11",
    "type": "building_spawned",
    "source": "lunar_frontiers",
    "datacontenttype": "application/json",
    "time": "2023-07-30T18:07:40.210505Z",
    "data": {
      "game_id": "9c0562bb-6657-4918-ad21-bec63f38bc10",
      "site_id": "193e4856-3ffa-4509-b6b0-16f2d106d046",
      "site_type": "HQ",
      . . .
    }
  }
```

Here, the source field contains the name of the application. This doesn't utilize the field to its fullest. A far better use for this field is identifying the *exact* source of the cloud event: the user or entity responsible for producing it. If you require and know the identity of the event generator, then you can use it in the source field. For example, you might use user:1234 to identify the specific application user responsible for the event.

In many cases, events are produced by other components that may not have originated with some user-generated stimulus and that's fine. In these scenarios, you may want to simply provide the component name that produced the event. If a bearer token or some other proof was provided, you can store that in the event source or add it to a custom metadata field. In very secure environments, you may even see cryptographic signatures required to verify the authenticity of the source.

Let's see what such an event might look like:

```
{
    "specversion": "1.0",
    "id": "2a0562bb-6657-4918-ad21-bec63f38bc11",
    "type": "building_spawned",
    "source": "eyJhbGciOiJIUzI1NiIsInR5cC...xk",
    "datacontenttype": "application/json",
```

```
  "time": "2023-07-30T18:07:40.210505Z",
  "data": {
    "game_id": "9c0562bb-6657-4918-ad21-bec63f38bc10",
    "site_id": "193e4856-3ffa-4509-b6b0-16f2d106d046",
    "site_type": "HQ",
    . . .
  }
}
```

To keep that listing printable in this book, the JSON Web Token or "bearer" token has been trimmed. If you want to examine the contents of the full token, you can access it on the JWT site.[4] By storing the bearer token used at the time of event writing directly on the event, you have full access to audit information on that event and writes can be limited to any client that passes your own authorization and identity checks.

JSON Web Tokens aren't the only tokens that can be stored in the source field. A popular (but arguably more complicated) means of identifying *client workloads* is SPIFFE (Secure Production Identity Framework for Everyone).[5]

JWTs and SPIFFE identity tokens are only the tip of the iceberg. Many organizations use their own proprietary tokens, and others are adopting formats like macaroons[6] that used to be seen as esoteric or academic. The only real requirement is that the token you use should be *freestanding*. In other words, the means to view, identify, and verify the security context can't be something that relies on ephemeral data or information that could lose meaning over time. You should get the same audit result for a given event today as you do three years from now.

The choice of what token or data you use is entirely up to you based on your own circumstances. But putting some kind of authorization and authentication token on the event indicating the information used to make the "can this client write an event?" decision can be invaluable and usually doesn't require much extra effort or code to implement.

Securing Command Paths

It's worth remembering that *commands don't exist.*[7] They're short-lived requests made to an aggregate. If the command is accepted, then the aggregate

---

4.   https://jwt.io/#debugger-io?token=eyJhbGciOiJIUzI1NiIsInR5cCI6IkpXVCJ9.eyJzdWIiOiIxMjM0NTY3ODkwIi-wibmFtZSI6IkV2ZW50IEluamVjdG9yIiwiaWF0IjoxNTE2MjM5MDIyfQ.rQZYkUAWoSoyjHV1Z_Ity0p-Fm38QD5E0vFxiaeBXxk

5.   https://spiffe.io

6.   https://research.google/pubs/pub41892/

7.   https://cosmonic.com/blog/engineering/commands-are-not-real

will emit the corresponding events. Reality hasn't been affected until something emits an event.

This means that securing the command path becomes very much like securing access to a microservice (and many organizations and libraries actually use microservices as the entry point for commands). You'll want to be certain that only those entities authorized to submit commands to your application can do so. No matter what identity is responsible for submitting a command, *nothing* should be able to bypass the validation performed by the aggregate.

Securing microservices is well beyond the scope of this book, but you could opt for something as simple as HTTP basic authentication or use bearer tokens. One important thing to keep in mind when securing microservices is that authorization isn't the same thing as authentication. The first deals with determining *what* a user can do while the latter is concerned with *who* the user claims to be. An open technology standard like OAuth is a favorite among microservice developers.

The means by which clients authenticate to a command service doesn't have to be the same as the authentication mechanism anywhere else in the system.

Securing Projections and Component State

Securing projections as well as aggregate and process manager state is a relatively straightforward process. You'll need to ensure that only the authorized components can read from and write to the various data stores. In an ideal world, each one of them will have their own unique authentication which would prevent lateral escalation attacks if someone compromised only one component.

Securing these types of data depends almost entirely on the application or platform you're using to store that data. Most data stores have, at the very least, credentials-based authentication, and many have robust authentication and authorization schemes.

As you set out to design and build your application and you're evaluating data stores for storing and retrieving state, make sure you do some research and compare the security and authentication features and not only performance and developer experience.

Supporting GDPR and the Right to Be Forgotten

GDPR, or the *General Data Protection Regulation*, exerts an awful lot of influence on how backends, data storage plans, cloud architecture, and more are all designed. This regulation is pretty lengthy if you're interested in reading all of it, but the parts of it that apply to this chapter are articles 17 and 19, or the "right to erasure."[8] In short, customers have the right to demand that all of their information be erased or forgotten. Failing to comply with a request like this can result in hefty fines.

While GDPR is specifically a European Union regulation, organizations in the United States and many other countries often follow it because of its clarity and rigorous rules. This is especially important for companies that host services and store data in multiple countries while their users reside in other countries with varying local regulations. In most cases, GDPR is the most strict, so embracing it by default can be beneficial and time-saving.

This next section discusses how you can support a customer's right to data erasure while still maintaining the immutability of the event stream.

Crypto-Shredding

Historically, shredding documents in a physical machine that cut up paper was a way of safely disposing of secure information (like *PII*, or *Personally Identifiable Information*). Depending on the nature of the organization, it was also a helpful way of disposing of crucial evidence of crimes before the authorities arrived.

Crypto-shredding is a technique that can be used to effectively dispose of PII while not violating the first law of event sourcing: *events are immutable*. When a user exercises their right to be forgotten, it's our legal responsibility to ensure that their data has indeed been "forgotten." Thankfully, forgetting can be done without deleting events from the stream.

Shredding in this context refers to disposing of (or forgetting) a private key that's required to decrypt sensitive information on an event.

Let's take a look at an event in Cloud Events JSON format that has data on it that qualifies as PII:

```
{
    "specversion": "1.0",
    "id": "2a0562bb-6657-4918-ad21-bec63f38bc11",
    "type": "funds_withdrawn",
    "source": "eyJhbGciOiJIUzI1NiIsInR5cC...xk",
    "datacontenttype": "application/json",
    "time": "2023-07-30T18:07:40.210505Z",
    "data": {
```

---

8.   https://www.dataprotection.ie/en/individuals/know-your-rights/right-erasure-articles-17-19-gdpr

```
    "account_number": "3BR5679DF",
    "amount": 2300
    . . .
  }
}
```

This event contains an unmodified account number. This qualifies as PII and needs to be included in the list of data removed as part of any GDPR article 17 or 19 (the right to erasure) request. It's also sensitive enough that you might not want to leave it lying around in plain text even in your event log.

This account number can be encrypted and placed on the event. When setting a system up for crypto-shredding, PII reference IDs are often used to identify the owner of the encryption key. In the preceding funds_withdrawn event, the account number is 3BR5679DF, but that's likely one of many accounts owned by the user whose data falls under GDPR jurisdiction.

Here you would assign this customer a PII reference ID that's completely opaque and on its own contains nothing that could be used to refer back to a human. This reference ID is essentially a lookup into a table of keys or some secure storage service like HashiCorp Vault.[9]

The new, secure event might look something like this:

```
{
    "specversion": "1.0",
    "id": "2a0562bb-6657-4918-ad21-bec63f38bc11",
    "x-pii-reference-key": "30a584ae-4c80-4056-baf2-1d2b0a1c4bf3",
    "type": "funds_withdrawn",
    "source": "eyJhbGciOiJIUzI1NiIsInR5cC...xk",
    "datacontenttype": "application/json",
    "time": "2023-07-30T18:07:40.210505Z",
    "data": {
      "account_number": " ... encrypted data ... ",
      "amount": 2300,
      "memo": "this is the best application ever"
      . . .
    }
}
```

Note the use of an extension header (x-pii-reference-key) to add that metadata to the event header. Putting it in the header like this can be helpful for a number of reasons, especially if you need to scan an entire event stream for a given PII reference.

_____

9. https://www.vaultproject.io

Another pattern you might notice here is that the entire payload hasn't been encrypted. In an immutable event log, even if the customer that owns the referenced account has been forgotten, the indisputable fact that *someone* withdrew $2300 on that date and time can't be forgotten. Using some means external to the event stream itself, your application will need to identify the relevant PII fields so it knows which ones to encrypt. JSON schema supports this natively while other schema languages might need extensions (for example, protobufs support arbitrary metadata which can include PII flags).

When we crypto-shred this customer, the private key corresponding to their PII reference is removed and the sensitive information is no longer available to the customer or the application.

Supporting Retention Periods

Crypto-shredding can also be used to support automatic retention periods (and subsequent forgetting of expired data). Double encryption is a handy way of dealing with this requirement. You still maintain the PII reference key for the sensitive data, but that data is then encrypted a second time using an expiring "retention period" key. If the sensitive information is *renewed*, then the outer layer is decrypted and then re-encrypted with a new retention period key.

The following diagram illustrates how sensitive information subject to retention regulations might be stored in an event:

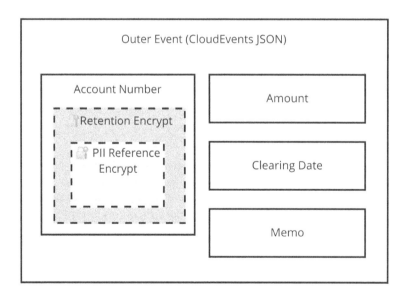

The possibilities are endless, but it's typically a trivial amount of book-keeping to associate the retention period key with the same entity as the PII reference key. Many key store applications can help you do this automatically by setting up key hierarchies and associations that are only visible inside the secure vault.

Rationalizing Crypto-Shredding with External Context

If something about the use of outside encryption keys bothers you, that's a good thing. Throughout this entire book, you've learned that events must stand alone and that no action can be taken on the event that requires information that's *not on the event*.

Think of an event log that must store global financial transactions. The context that must reside in the event is the exchange rate *at the time of the event*. Otherwise, a transaction's meaning (and dollar value) could change over time, causing all sorts of problems. Without this embedded context, processing the event log won't be deterministic.

Another way to think about this is that some information on events can refer to other things, even if the reference itself is opaque. A unique ID in an event field that refers to an entity not established by previous events is still a valid unique ID and (depending on the modeling domain) may not be considered a side effect. It might feel like we're skating by on a technicality there, but that's where the rationale comes from.

The string 3BR5679DF and the string fsdjlkcam843fnsa= can be considered logically identical; the only real difference is that the second information has had an encoding protocol applied to it. It's like base64 encoding a field. It's still the same data underneath, and the encoding has simply been applied to fit a specific purpose.

In this case, we're actually banking on the mutability of the external data. We *want* the private key to be one that can go away forever, thereby shredding the sensitive data on the event. If you decide to implement crypto-shredding and your team is new to event sourcing, you might want to document somewhere how the use of PII references to externally stored private keys isn't a violation of any of the event sourcing laws.

Wrapping Up

In this chapter, you explored the different zones of security in an event-sourced application as well as techniques and patterns that can be used to secure each of those. Security should never be an afterthought, and it's well worth figuring out your security posture before you start filling up your event stream.

In the next chapter, you'll learn how to perform manual and automated testing on event-sourced applications. Many developers consider testing to be one of event sourcing's underrated super powers. Few things are as satisfying as the level of confidence you can get from a well-built event sourcing test suite.

## CHAPTER 9

Testing Event-Sourced Systems

Now that you've experienced the core building blocks of event-sourced applications from writing code to securing systems, it's time to start thinking about how this works on teams, at scales, and in production.

For that, you'll need to test. The ability to reliably and easily test an application is one of the core reasons why people embrace event sourcing as a pattern. Unfortunately, testing is one of the least documented and discussed aspects of event sourcing. This leaves us with a dichotomy: it should be easy, but we don't know how to do it.

In this chapter, you'll see that testing event-sourced applications *should be* as simple as writing tests for pure functions. You'll also see that you can use this as a litmus test to verify your models and even vet the tooling and development frameworks you're using on a daily basis.

Testing Aggregates

Aggregates accept commands and, depending on their current state, will return 0 or more events. As a pure function, this looks like the following:

```
f(state, command) = e1 ... en
```

As a result, it should be easy to write tests that supply scenario states and commands and assert the results. One of the most common failures in aggregate testing comes from the aggregate reaching outside of the event stream for additional metadata such as a running clock.

Countless automated testing frameworks exist that have their own advantages and disadvantages. The criteria for picking a testing framework to test your aggregates is that it should be *easy* to test your aggregate's pure functions. This comes with an implicit requirement that you be able to invoke a pure function for the aggregate under test—a requirement that you need to satisfy by choosing the right separation of concerns in your code. Separating the pure logic from whatever eventing framework you're using will pay massive dividends throughout the life of your application.

Take a look at the following (simplified) Elixir test that performs assertions against some pure functions that reside in an aggregate module. Note that there's no evidence of any event sourcing framework or the Commanded library anywhere.

```elixir
defmodule AggregateTest do
  use ExUnit.Case

  test "produces overdraft event on negative balance" do
    state = %{balance: 50, account_number: "B00100"}
    cmd = %Bank.WithdrawCommand{account_number: "B00100", amount: 100}

    assert BankAggregate.handle_command(state, cmd) == [
      %{
        event_type: :amount_withdrawn,
        amount: 100,
        account_number: "B00100",
        effective_balance: -50
      },
      %{
        event_type: :overdraft,
        account_number: "B00100",
        overage: 50
      }
    ]
  end
end
```

Continuing the bank account example, you would also want to write tests that assert that deposits and transfers work properly and that edge cases like withdrawals from overdrawn accounts are prevented, and so on.

Note that the handle_command function in the BankAggregate module is a pure function that takes in state and a command and returns events. There is no tight coupling with any specific framework or library. Writing functions like this that can then be called by higher-level frameworks and libraries helps keep the event sourcing promise of easy testing.

With that, it would be easy to assume that the next thing to test is applying events to the aggregate to ensure that its state is correct:

```
f(state, event) = state'
```

Unfortunately, this is a trap that needs to be avoided, which brings us to the next unchangeable law: "Never Test Internal State."

Never Test Internal State

 Internal state of aggregates and process managers can change in form and purpose. Tests should supply input and assert output without enforcing or asserting the shape of internal state.

Does it matter to us how the aggregate manages its internal state? Or, is the important thing that when commands are applied to an aggregate, the right events are returned? The events are the only aggregate output that matters to tests.

In an ideal testing environment, the test code never actually sees what the internal state of the aggregate looks like; it merely holds onto it like an opaque token. Let's rewrite the previous test with an eye toward keeping the aggregate state inside a black box:

```elixir
defmodule AggregateTest do
  use ExUnit.Case

  test "produces overdraft event on negative balance" do
    initial_state = BankAccount.new("B00100")

    events = BankAccount.handle_command(
      initial_state,
      %Bank.Deposit{account_number: "B00100", amount: 50}
    )
    state1 = BankAccount.apply_events(initial_state, events)
    events2 = BankAccount.handle_command(
      state1,
      %Bank.Withdraw{account_number: "B00100", amount: 100}
    )

    assert events2 == [
      %{
        event_type: :amount_withdrawn,
        amount: 100,
        account_number: "B00100",
        effective_balance: -50
      },
      %{
        event_type: :overdraft,
        account_number: "B00100",
        overage: 50
      }
    ]
  end
end
```

In this code, the state is created through an aggregate constructor but the test doesn't care about its shape. Next, a set of commands is applied, and events are asserted without the test inspecting the internal state variable.

Events and commands represent a fixed, public API while internal state can change over time so long as it doesn't break the tests.

Note that the new aggregate state is produced through the apply_events call and not fabricated manually by the test itself.

You could easily refactor this Elixir code into a nice fold over a series of commands, but it's been broken out here to make the logic easy to follow.

Testing Projectors

Projectors produce *external* state, or state that's designed to be consumed by third parties. Since this state is part of the public API of the system, you need to write tests that assert that the shape of the projections matches what you expect.

It's tempting to have your projector write the projected state directly to the external data store. When building examples and prototypes, it's often much easier to simply write the projection out during processing. But when it comes time to test, such a design pattern makes the projector "effectful." Writing the data ends up being a side effect of processing events.

It's much more testable (and arguably cleaner) if the projectors *return* the new projection as a result of processing events, and some other entity in your application is then responsible for persisting that projection. This is potentially more difficult because it forces you to design your projection as a single object, whereas if you were writing directly to a database, you could split it into multiple tables or even across multiple databases.

If you want to build testable projectors, then the way in which projections are persisted should be completely separate from the projection itself. Take a look at the following code that tests a bank account projector:

```elixir
defmodule ProjectorTest do
  use ExUnit.Case

  test "projector subtracts withdrawals" do
    projection = BankAccountProjection.empty()
    evts = [
      %{event_type: :account_created, account_number: "B00100"},
      %{event_type: :amount_deposited, account_number: "B00100", amount: 500}
    ]
    projection2 = BankAccountProjection.apply_events(projection, evts)
    assert projection2 == %{
      account_number: "B00100",
      balance: 500
    }
  end
end
```

In this example, the bank account projection has access to the current projection when applying a new event. This lets the projector do things like adding and subtracting amounts from a running balance when it applies events. *However*, this isn't the cleanest way to model this.

Requiring a projector to have access to previous versions of itself can create an unnecessary burden on the system, and it can also open it up to consistency problems at scale. If a large number of transactions are occurring simultaneously, it can be easy to confuse a projection by giving it the wrong data for its previous version. Sure, you can counter this with things like version numbers on the projection, but in many cases, you don't need this complexity.

When evaluating any event sourcing framework, you'll want to verify that it provides consistency or atomicity guarantees around projections and projection updates. If you can't get these guarantees, then you may want to consider a different framework or refactoring your model.

Let's take a look at an alternate way you can model events if you can't guarantee the reliability of transactional projection updates:

```
defmodule ProjectorTest do
  use ExUnit.Case

  test "projector subtracts withdrawals - take 2" do
    evts = [
      %{event_type: :account_created, account_number: "B00100"},
      %{event_type: :amount_deposited, account_number: "B00100",
        amount: 500,
        effective_balance: 500}
    ]
  end
end
```

Here, the effective_balance field is produced by the aggregate so the projector doesn't need to read a previous version of itself to calculate this.

Opinion warning: You may be completely fine with projectors accessing their previous versions while someone else may not. Regardless of how you feel about this, making sure that everyone knows the guarantees (or lack thereof) that your platform supports is critical.

This level of projector isolation "purity" isn't always possible or even practical. Recall the example of a leaderboard from the earlier chapters. If you have a leaderboard aggregate that's emitting LeaderBoardUpdated events, then the projectors can be blissfully unaware of history, and only produce projections based on isolated events.

If you don't have such a leaderboard aggregate, then the projection will have to maintain the top n scores for a given leaderboard and will need access to the previous leaderboard whenever it applies a ScoreChanged event.

You can see how, in JavaScript projectors, EventStoreDB automatically gives a projection access to its previous value. This works well for event store because it can guarantee the consistency of the projection state since it controls event delivery to projectors.

Testing Process Managers

Process managers are the inverse of aggregates. A process manager ingests events and produces commands that can either advance or terminate a process. This means that the pure function for a process manager is this:

```
f(state, event) = c0...cn
```

The process manager is given its state and a new event and it can then return 0 or more commands. Let's take a look at an example from a variant of Lunar Frontiers where you want to ensure that the construction process manager requests the spawning of a new building when a construction site is finished.

```
defmodule ConstructionProcessTest do
  use ExUnit.Case

  test "process manager spawns buildings" do
    input = %{event_type: :construction_completed,
             site_x: 0,
             site_y: 2,
             owner: "bob",
             site_type: :barracks}

    assert ConstructionManager.handle_event(%{}, input) ==
      %SpawnBuilding{
        building_type: :barracks,
        x: 0,
        y: 2,
        owner: "bob"
      }
  end
end
```

Remember that the commands are supplied to aggregates, and the aggregates are then responsible for validating those commands against current state. This means that the aggregate can reject a SpawnBuilding command if the colony lacks sufficient resources to build it, the site is no longer viable, or the colony is under attack—the possibilities are endless. The important part is that the command validation is done by the aggregates, and process advancement or termination is done by the process managers.

Put another way, the process manager doesn't decide whether it's possible to spawn a new building. It emits the SpawnBuilding command and lets the rest of the machinery deal with it. This narrow separation of concerns can take a while to get used to, but writing tests for it can help maintain a mental model.

With simple events and commands like this, it's easy to think that this might be overkill. In the early days of any event-sourced application, that's generally how people feel. Then, when people start modeling and testing more complicated logic, the benefits of the clear and enforced boundaries pay off many times over.

Event-sourced systems are massive domino arrangements, awaiting a single piece to fall for a complex pattern to emerge. But testing that each miniscule piece behaves according to plan doesn't mean you can get away without writing holistic tests.

Using Automated and Acceptance Testing

So far, you've written tests that ensure that aggregates do what they're supposed to, that projectors behave properly, and that process managers issue the right commands. The next step up is to test the choreography of the complex dance that's an event-sourced application.

A common mistake in writing acceptance or integration tests (the debate over these categories, their names, and what belongs in them will continue until the end of time) is testing too much. If you already know that your aggregate produces the right events, do you also need to write a higher-level flow test that ensures that you have the right events?

It's worth taking a step back and looking at *why* you need holistic flow tests. Firstly, you shouldn't be testing that dispatch actually happens, since that should be done as part of whatever framework you're using. Secondly, if you're following the laws of event sourcing, you shouldn't make any assertions about *internal* state of aggregates or process managers.

What you're looking for are logic flaws—some failure to produce the desired result under some simulated flow of events and commands through the system. What happens most often here is you write the "script" for the holistic test, and it fails. You then go back and realize that a test passed in an aggregate or process manager when it shouldn't have. You refactor the behavior and then the tests turn green.

Without these higher-level tests, you won't be able to find the logic flaws in individual components that appear to be passing tests in isolation.

Let's take a look at some code (actually unlikely-to-compile pseudocode) that illustrates the flow you want to assert:

```
defmodule ProjectorTest do
  use ExUnit.Case

  test "new player flow" do
    cmds = [
      create_game(),
      create_player(),
      advance_turns(5)
    ]
    Flow.inject(cmds)

    assert_event :game_created
    assert_event :player_created
    assert_event :construction_advanced, 4
    assert_event :construction_completed
    assert_event :building_spawned, &(:building_type == :headquarters)
  end
end
```

What you're looking for here is that after creating a player and 5 turns pass by, that player has received a new headquarters. It's entirely possible that all of the aggregates, projectors, and process managers could pass their tests in isolation and this flow test fails. If this flow test fails, it's likely because of incorrect logic in one of the components. The flow tests surface these bugs and let you refactor them now rather than when horrible bugs happen in production (but, because we're using event sourcing, production bugs are usually only a replay away from being fixed).

Note that you didn't need to assert that a specific set of commands was generated by the process manager. That's covered in the process manager's unit test, and this flow will fail if there's a flaw in that logic. For example, if the process manager never emitted a SpawnBuilding command and yet still passed its unit tests, this flow would fail and you'd know why.

These kinds of high-level scripts describing deep and potentially complex flows are often huge sources of friction for teams building traditional applications. Running and automating these scripts can actually be a pleasant or even fun exercise with event-sourced applications.

Wrapping Up

This chapter was less about testing than it was about test system requirements. If your library and tooling don't make testing an event-sourced application easy, then you may want to look for a different framework.

Structuring your code so that you separate the pure functions of business logic from the dispatch, coding, and encoding work of event sourcing also makes it easy to test your applications.

Finally, you also saw that in addition to testing all of your components in isolation, you'll want to test long flows that your application needs to support. This will surface logic bugs in the individual components or highlight problems with your expectations of flows.

Testing is one of the main reasons why people embrace event sourcing. Next, you're going to continue exploring how to build bigger and more complex systems by learning more about how to model, document, and discover event-sourced systems.

CHAPTER 10

Modeling Discoverable Application Domains

Many of the samples in this book have been presented in such a way that you could get a high-level overview of the event flow, event schemas, and command schemas with a quick review. In looking at the various versions of the Lunar Frontiers application, you can simply click in the aggregates, events, or commands folders and get a complete overview of how everything works.

Unfortunately, this isn't how the real world usually works. The real world has more depth, and this depth needs to be shared and understood by one or more teams collaborating on event-sourced applications. Some events may be shared across teams while others are only used within a single service or piece of the application. When the code base for an event-sourced application is distributed and managed across multiple teams, it becomes incredibly hard to have that comprehensive view of the application model. Organizations that have no single comprehensive view of an application's event model are commonplace.

In this chapter, you'll learn some techniques and tools for modeling that can help manage the chaos. In addition, you'll learn strategies for the single most important requirement for an application model: *keeping the model and the code in sync.*

This chapter is organized into two main sections. In the first section, you'll experience defining and documenting the schemas for individual events and commands. This defines the shape and size of the data exchanged between components: the list of fields and their data types. In the second section of the chapter, you'll add a higher level of modeling and document the flow of events and commands through a system.

Defining and Documenting Schemas

So far, the schema for the structures used by applications has been done without much fanfare. In the Lunar Frontiers application, the schemas are part of the structure definitions, such as this building spawned event:

```elixir
defmodule LunarFrontiers.App.Events.BuildingSpawned.V2 do
  @derive Jason.Encoder
  defstruct [:site_id,
             :game_id,
             :site_type,
             :location,
             :player_id,
             :tick,
             :completion_ticks]
end
```

Of course, this isn't truly a schema as much as it is a list of untyped fields. Elixir's relationship with strong typing is a complex one, but type specifications can be added to structures like this to give developers a better understanding of what's actually in an event. For example, you could add a type specification to this struct as follows:

```elixir
defmodule LunarFrontiers.App.Events.BuildingSpawned.V2 do
  @type t :: %__MODULE__{
          site_id:   String.t,
          game_id: String.t,
          site_type: :oxygen_generator |
                     :water_generator  |
                     :hq               |
                     :power_generator  |
                     :colonist_housing,
          location: Point.t,
          player_id: String.t,
          tick: integer,
          completion_ticks: integer
        }

  @enforce_keys [:site_id, :game_id, :site_type]

  @derive Jason.Encoder
  defstruct [:site_id,
             :game_id,
             :site_type,
             :location,
             :player_id,
             :tick,
             :completion_ticks]
end
```

This is definitely a step in the right direction. Now anyone looking at the code can tell at a glance what the various fields are for, their data types, and the list of valid values for site_type. This is great for developers, but it doesn't solve the discoverability and documentation problem for other stakeholders. People who might not be heads-down in the code every day still need to be able to reason about events, commands, and flows without searching through the code.

When you need the schemas to be visible outside the code (or your development language is so loosely typed that you can't embed schemas), the next reasonable step is to take a look at various *Domain Specific Languages* (*DSLs*)[1] for schema definition.

A seemingly infinite number of schema definition languages exist, so there's no way this book could cover all of them. In this section, we'll go through some of the most common and popular, especially within the event sourcing community.

Modeling with JSON Schemas

A *JSON Schema*[2] is a declarative language (represented with JSON) that annotates and validates JSON documents. If you intend to represent your events and commands in your system as JSON documents, then defining schemas as JSON Schema documents makes sense. While not the most human-friendly language, JSON is still readable, but, more importantly, it can be read and processed by any language that can read JSON. It's also ubiquitous these days that all the major languages have libraries for parsing JSON schemas and validating documents against those schemas.

The following is an example of a JSON schema for the BuildingSpawned event (some of the properties have been left out to keep things readable):

```
{
  "$schema": "https://json-schema.org/draft/2020-12/schema",
  "$id": "https://lunarfrontiers.com/schema/events/building_spawned.json",
  "title": "BuildingSpawned",
  "description": "An event indicating a building spawned",
  "type": "object",
  "properties": {
    "site_id": {
      "description": "A UUID for the site",
      "type": "string"
    },
```

---

1.   https://martinfowler.com/dsl.html
2.   https://json-schema.org

```
    "site_type": {
      "description": "The type of this building",
      "type": "string",
      "enum": ["HQ", "OxygenGenerator", "WaterGenerator", "Housing"]
    },

    . . .

  }
}
```

JSON schemas, being written as JSON documents, are one of the more easily used schema formats. JSON schemas make it easy to embed documentation in the model, and they also act as a source for generating markdown documentation and application code.

Modeling with Protocol Buffers

Protocol buffers[3] are a language- and platform-neutral way of describing and serializing data. Protocol buffers, often simply referred to as *protobufs*, provide a way of serializing data as compact binary payloads for transmission over a network and they also provide a means of describing the schema via a Schema Definition Language (SDL).

One of the fun bits of trivia about protobufs is that a ready-made protobuf *message* (think "struct" or "record") exists that defines a protobuf schema. A powerful and subtle feature of protobuf schemas is that they can be serialized and transmitted the same way regular messages can. This also helps keep you within the walled garden boundaries of the protobuf ecosystem, since you use protobufs both for serializing and describing messages.

The following is an example of a protobuf (.proto) file describing the BuildingSpawned event as a message:

```
chap11/buildingspawned.proto
syntax = "proto3";

enum SiteType {
  HQ = 0;
  OXYGEN_GENERATOR = 1;
  WATER_GENERATOR = 2;
  POWER_GENERATOR = 3;
}

message Point {
  uint32 x = 1;
  uint32 y = 2;
}
```

3. https://protobuf.dev

```
message BuildingSpawned {
  string site_id = 1;
  string game_id = 2;
  SiteType site_type = 3;
  Point location = 4;
  string player_id = 5;
  uint64 ticks = 6;
  uint32 completion_ticks = 7;
}
```

To work with protobufs, you'll want to make sure that you've installed the protoc application suitable for your CPU architecture and OS. Then, you'll be able to use that CLI to generate code in any number of languages based on this schema, as well as perform a handful of testing and diagnostics functions.

If you want to generate the C# code necessary to encode and decode this event, you can use the protoc CLI as follows:

```
protoc buildingspawned.proto --csharp_out=.
```

This generates *a lot* of code. Rather than wasting dozens of pages listing it all out, take a look at a small snippet from the generated C# code for the SiteType enum. You can see that it's using some annotations to tag the C# enum with the original values from the protobuf file.

```
public enum SiteType {
  [pbr::OriginalName("HQ")] Hq = 0,
  [pbr::OriginalName("OXYGEN_GENERATOR")] OxygenGenerator = 1,
  [pbr::OriginalName("WATER_GENERATOR")] WaterGenerator = 2,
  [pbr::OriginalName("POWER_GENERATOR")] PowerGenerator = 3,
}
```

Every language is different, but nearly all of them generate an enormous amount of code meant for consumption rather than reading or understanding directly. Out of the box, protoc supports C++, C#, Java, Kotlin, Objective-C, PHP, Python, and Ruby, and there's even an experimental flag for Rust. If your favorite language isn't included by default (for example, Go), you can probably find a protoc plugin that does what you need.

Modeling with Avro

Apache Avro[4] is a topic big enough for a book all on its own. Avro is a data serialization system. You define how data is serialized through Avro schemas, but Avro also has tons of other features, including allowing for the definition of remote procedure calls.

---

4.   https://avro.apache.org/docs/#schemas

If you choose Apache Kafka as a core part of your event platform, then you might end up using Avro schemas because Kafka supports it natively and the two technologies (Kafka and Avro) work well together.

Other ways to represent an Avro schema exist (such as JSON), but the easiest for humans to digest is Avro's Interface Definition Language (IDL). Here's a sample Avro schema defining the BuildingSpawned event:

```
enum SiteTypes {
  OXYGENERATOR, WATERGENERATOR, POWERGENERATOR, HQ, HOUSING
}
record BuildingSpawned {
  string site_id;
  string game_id;
  SiteTypes site_type;
  Point location;
  string player_id;
  int ticks;
  int completion_ticks;
}
```

In contrast to protobuf, Avro's documentation makes a point of calling out that it doesn't require code generation. Obviously, covering Avro and all its intricacies is beyond the scope of this book, so if the IDL looks appealing and you're potentially working within the Kafka ecosystem, you might want to explore it further.

Examining Cloud Events

As you saw in Chapter 3, Cloud Events[5] is a specification for defining events in a common way. Over the years, a number of common patterns have arisen for representing event data. The most common of these is the use of an *envelope*, which is an outer layer wrapping the event that contains metadata like the event type, timestamp, content type, origin, and so on.

The Cloud Events specification codifies this pattern into a standard that's now used in a number of applications and open source projects. Cloud events *do not* give you the tools to specify the schema of an event. They only provide a means to encapsulate or wrap the event data. You'll still need to use some other mechanism to externally document the schema.

---

5. https://cloudevents.io

The following is a sample JSON representation of a cloud event:

```
{
    "specversion": "1.0",
    "id": "2a0562bb-6657-4918-ad21-bec63f38bc11",
    "type": "building_spawned",
    "source": "lunar_frontiers",
    "datacontenttype": "application/json",
    "time": "2023-07-30T18:07:40.210505Z",
    "data": {
      "game_id": "9c0562bb-6657-4918-ad21-bec63f38bc10",
      "site_id": "193e4856-3ffa-4509-b6b0-16f2d106d046",
      "site_type": "HQ",
      . . .
    }
  }
```

The outer envelope includes several important key fields. The id field is often used in duplicate checking. The type field allows for content-based routing and decisions without needing to examine the data field. The source field is relatively free-form and is used to identify the message originator. Lastly, the inner payload, the data field, only needs to adhere to the envelope's declared mime type. In this case, it would be JSON. The data field can be any number of representations, but regular JSON is among the easiest to use.

Cloud events can be represented in any number of formats beyond JSON, including Avro[6] and Protocol Buffers.[7]

Deciding on an Event Schema Language

You're the only one who can decide which language or toolset you're going to use to define your event schema. Your choice depends a lot on whether your organization already has an existing investment in certain technologies like JSON schema, protobufs, Avro, and so on and also on the personal preferences of team members.

When deciding on a language, make sure that it's one that you can incorporate into your automated tooling and that it fits well with what you decide to use to model the *flows* (discussed next).

---

6. https://github.com/cloudevents/spec/blob/v1.0.2/cloudevents/formats/avro-format.md
7. https://github.com/cloudevents/spec/blob/v1.0.2/cloudevents/formats/protobuf-format.md

Modeling Event Flows

What the schema definition languages *don't* provide is a way of visualizing and documenting the flow of events and commands through the system. They let you declare the fields and data types on events and commands, but nothing is built into any of these formats for defining flows.

Any event-sourced system of a complexity larger than "hello world" will come with an intrinsic lack of visibility into how events and commands flow through the system. This will be *especially* true for process managers. While you can look at the code for an individual process manager to see what it does, you're not going to want to keep refreshing your memory every few months by re-reading the code for dozens of process managers. This also won't help the stakeholders and teammates who can't easily read the code.

Event Flows Are Directed Graphs

When we describe event sourcing flows, we use phrases like "the aggregate emits the funds withdrawn event" or "the projector consumes the funds withdrawn event." Words like *emits* and *consumes* should provide a hint that an event-sourced application flow can be distilled down to a *directed graph.* Let's take a look at a few graphs.

In this first graph, everything is simple and easy to read. The aggregate is at the center of the flow with commands coming in and events going out. What isn't represented in this graph is the fact that some (or all) of the events an aggregate emits come back to that same aggregate so it can update its internal state.

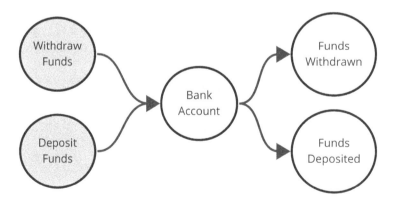

Now, let's take a look at another graph. This time, the graph includes a projector and a process manager for the bank account entity. We've only added two additional components and the graph is already chaotic. You can imagine what it would be like to try and visualize an entire application with dozens of aggregates, process managers, and projectors. It's a nightmare—the very nightmare that inspired (terrified?) me to include this chapter in the book.

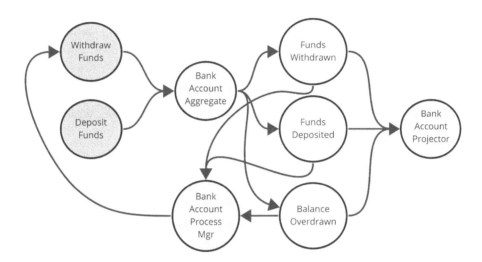

The downside of manually managing these graphs is that they can quickly get incredibly dense and complicated. It takes a lot of work and some serious design acumen to keep these diagrams from degrading into spaghetti. While graphs do a good job of illustrating flows, there's no room for documentation or schema specification.

In the next few sections, you'll see some tools and applications that can alleviate the burden of manually drawing graphs and hopefully provide a solution that gives you graphs, documentation, and schemas.

Specifying Systems with AsyncAPI

AsyncAPI[8] refers to a specification and set of tools for defining asynchronous APIs. It's a general-purpose specification that lets you define your application in terms of asynchronous APIs and some basic building blocks. Because the specification is general-purpose, you'll notice a bit of a gap exists between AsyncAPI and strict event sourcing terminology.

---

8. https://www.asyncapi.com

An AsyncAPI document is made up of some or all of the following:

- *Server*—A server is a broker system responsible for connecting consumers and producers.

- *Producer*—A producer is an application (AsyncAPI interprets the word "application" broadly) that publishes messages.

- *Consumer*—A consumer is an application that listens for events.

- *Channel*—A channel is the *means* by which messages flow through servers between producers and consumers. Channels in this specification can represent concepts like topics, queues, routes, paths, or subjects depending on which protocols are used.

- *Application*—An application is a broad category that can be a program or collection of programs. This can be a microservice, groups of microservices, a monolith, an IoT sensor, and so on.

- *Protocol*—Protocols define *how* information flows through the system. Note that you can still specify your system even if you don't use any of the predefined protocols.

- *Message*—A message is a unit of data transmitted from a producer to a consumer through a server.

AsyncAPI documents can be YAML or a subset of JSON, but YAML tends to be a bit easier for people to read. Take a look at the following specification:

```yaml
asyncapi: 2.5.0
info:
  title: Bank
  version: 0.1.0
channels:
  bank/funds-withdrawn:
    subscribe:
      message:
        description: An event indicating funds withdrawn from an account
        payload:
          type: object
          additionalProperties: false
          properties:
            accountNumber:
              type: string
            routing:
              type: string
            amount:
              type: integer
              minimum: 1
```

Something that takes a bit of getting used to with AsyncAPI is the relative *direction* of the publish and subscribe elements. In the preceding YAML, it might be easy to think that the Bank API subscribes to the funds-withdrawn event. But the subscription here is actually from the perspective of the *client*. To put it more simply: *the Bank API offers the bank/funds-withdrawn event for subscription*. Similarly, if you see a publish in this file, it means that *clients* can publish *to* the API.

If you can describe your application in terms of AsyncAPI primitives, then it can be an incredibly powerful tool to combine documentation and schemas into a single specification that can then be fed into tools and code generators.

I would recommend taking a small piece of your application and trying to model it out using AsyncAPI as an experiment to get a feel for it before deciding to model an entire project.

Documenting Systems with Event Catalog

Thinking back to the chaos inherent in even the simplest of flow visualizations, it's easy to see how many other problems spiral outward from that core. When someone changes the flow so that a process manager no longer handles an event or another process manager handles new events, an aggregate handles a few new commands, and the slightest change will immediately invalidate your diagrams. Keeping the diagrams and code in sync can end up being a full-time job for many people.

If you're also maintaining documentation, that usually becomes outdated as soon as the document is saved. One of the hardest things to do in event sourcing might not be writing the code, but ensuring that your code, flow visualizations, and documentation are all in sync.

Event Catalog[9] may be a way to solve that problem. It's an open source product that generates static websites. But these are no average sites: they have 3D graph visualizations, interactive and filterable node visualizers of applications, and even subdomains, as well as a way to store and visualize JSON schemas corresponding to messages.

---

9.   https://www.eventcatalog.dev

Here's an example showing a list of events in a system:

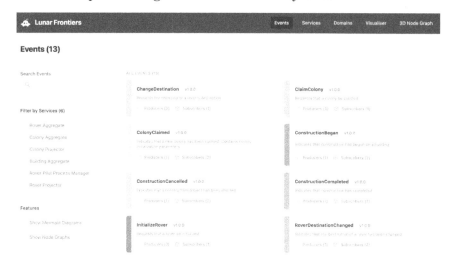

This image shows the 3D node visualizer in action:

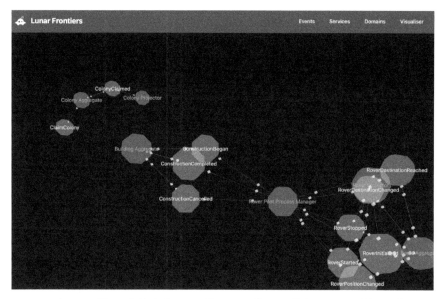

If you were to use Event Catalog on its own for nothing more than documentation and visualization, it could have a huge impact on the quality of life for developers in your team. But you can also do some clever things with Event Catalog.

First, the application has support for import plugins that allow it to ingest data from other sources, including AsyncAPI files. Second, if you look closely at the front matter in the markup files, you'll see that you have enough information to use Event Catalog as a code generation source:

```
---
name: RoverDestinationChanged
summary: "Indicates that the destination of a rover has been changed"
version: 1.0.0
producers:
    - 'Rover Aggregate'
consumers:
    - 'Rover Aggregate'
    - 'Rover Projector'
    - 'Rover Pilot Process Manager'
externalLinks: []
tags:
    - label: 'event'
badges: []
---
Some description goes here
```

I strongly recommend trying out Event Catalog. This is as easy to use as other static site generators like Hugo and Jekyll, but it's tailored to the needs of an organization wanting to document and drive collaboration around their event-driven applications. Event Catalog is also well structured enough that it can even be used as source material for "documentation-driven development." I was able to write a code generator for an event sourcing library that has tools that ingest Event Catalog sites for generating WebAssembly-based aggregates, process managers, and projectors.

Specifying Systems with RDF

If you aren't getting what you need from AsyncAPI, Event Catalog, or other tools, then graph databases might be your ally of last resort. Many of them, including the ever-popular Neo4j, include tools that dynamically render and visualize graphs and graph queries. So, if you're representing your event sourcing flow as data within a graph database, you get visualization (and some documentation) for free. You might be able to feed the graph data into a code generator to ensure that the code and graph always match.

There are other ways of representing graphs outside of native databases that can leverage entire ecosystems of tooling and support. For example, *RDF* (the *Resource Description Framework*),[10] which was originally designed as a way of exchanging data via the web, lets you compose *triples* from a subject, a predicate, and an object.

---

10. https://www.w3.org/TR/rdf11-concepts/

A graph in this format is a collection of triples—assertions of how nodes connect to each other. Subjects and objects form nodes while predicates create directed lines. The default way of representing RDF is through XML, making it extremely tool-friendly and barely human-friendly.

Luckily, a simpler way exists. *Turtle*[11] is a much more human-friendly (and yet still tool-friendly) way of representing a graph. It may not be as tailored to the domain as AsyncAPI or Event Catalog, but it can be the most precise.

The following snippet is taken from a W3C example that defines the relationships between Spider-Man and the Green Goblin:

```
<#green-goblin>
    rel:enemyOf <#spiderman> ;
    a foaf:Person ;     # in the context of the Marvel universe
    foaf:name "Green Goblin" .

<#spiderman>
    rel:enemyOf <#green-goblin> ;
    a foaf:Person ;
    foaf:name "Spiderman" .
```

You might decide to render this as shown in the following graph:

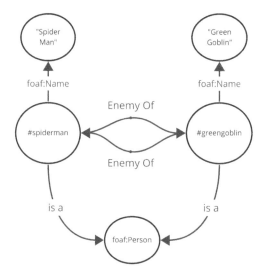

This is definitely more verbose with more nodes than you might think you need. But this Turtle format isn't only visualization-friendly, but also far more quarriable. Further, most graph databases are capable of emitting this kind of data either through an API call or through a user interface.

---

11. https://www.w3.org/TR/rdf12-turtle/

For additional reference, you can also take a look at auto-generated graph visualizations of Turtle documents rendered with a tool called *graphviz*.[12]

Modeling Case Study: Crafter Hustle

Designing and discovering event flows is like building a muscle. The more you exercise it, the stronger and better you get at it. I really enjoy this activity, especially when the domain is one that I don't deal with all the time. When I'm designing event flows for a developer-facing application or one in a domain like distributed systems, I can skip dozens of steps by having an internal monologue with myself as both the developer and the subject matter expert (SME).

But much of the time we may find ourselves modeling a domain in which we aren't the SME. I went through this exercise with someone recently and, even for a grizzled veteran like myself, I found the process enlightening. The application I modeled is called Crafter Hustle[13] and is designed to make life easier for people making and selling crafts through multiple channels.

Collect the Jobs to Be Done

The first thing I did was interview the SME, trying to tease out the *Jobs to Be Done (JTBD)*.[14] While the JTBD framework applies to more than applications, I find it helps me keep the user's perspective in the forefront.

The result of a lengthy back and forth with the SME resulted in the following high-level items:

- Keep track of supplies needed to make pieces of art

- Keep track of the art they have on hand

- Get useful information about going to craft shows to sell their wares. Specifically, was the profit worth the cost of being a vendor? They want to use that to figure out which shows to do next year.

- Manage consignments to different stores for different periods of time

- Track sales of art via online and direct sale

What's worth noting about this list is that it's free of technical jargon. These are the expert's words describing what the expert needs to do.

---

12. https://graphviz.org
13. https://crafterhustle.dev/docs
14. https://jobs-to-be-done.com

Establish a Common Language

When we're our own SME, it's easy to skip this step because we don't need a translator. But when you're working with SMEs who may not be technical at all, it's important to find a way to communicate so that both sides can understand each other. If I had to pick one aspect of building applications that's the most difficult, establishing a reliable and consistent common vocabulary between SMEs and software builders would be it.

In the interest of brevity, I will spare you the lengthy details and include here the terminology that I was able to glean. It might not mean much to you if you aren't a crafter, but that's rather the point. I had little knowledge of how any of this worked prior to going through the modeling process, and I was particularly surprised by how consignment works.

Inventory

Inventory refers to "stuff" the crafter has made that's in their possession (it doesn't matter where). These are finished products and *not* supplies used to make things. Each piece of inventory is considered unique, even if they've made a dozen of them.

Supplies

Supplies are consumed to make a product (which is in inventory). Some crafters, especially depending on the type of things they make, don't need to keep a tight track of supplies. Supplies might be cheap or easily obtained. In my SME's case, some of the supplies can be so expensive that they affect the bottom line and profit.

Show

A show is an event (not to be confused with an immutable piece of data that occurred in the past). A number of costs are associated with a show, including fees required to participate, travel, and materials that may only ever be used for shows (for example, a tent to cover a crafting "booth")

Consignment Merchant

A consignment merchant is a person or organization that takes artwork *on consignment*. This means that the crafter delivers inventory to the merchant and the merchant then sells the product. The merchant will take a small portion of the sale price as a way of leasing the space used by the crafter's products.

Consignment Period

Consignments aren't usually permanent. Most of the time, consignments have a period or a *run*. During the consignment period, the crafter's wares are on display and sold. The consignment period ends on a specific date or when all of the products have sold.

Custom Order

A custom order is when someone requests a certain type of craft. The customers can often specify details like their favorite colors or any number of options. Custom orders _reserve_ supplies until the crafter begins work on it, then the supplies are consumed to make a product.

With a common language and a list of requirements (for example, Jobs to be Done), I started to tease out a formal event model. You can even start to see the beginnings of some event flows in the definitions of the preceding nouns.

Discover Flows from the User's Perspective

Again to spare you all the boring details, I'll only illustrate one flow. I like to start with the hardest flow first, as I find that discoveries made during the most complex flow can make the remaining ones easier.

This flow describes the sequence of "events" as seen through the eyes of the user:

1. Make products (consume supplies)

2. Deliver products to consignment merchant (consignment period begins)

3. Merchant makes multiple sales of products; crafter may not know the details until the end of the period

4. Consignment period ends (merchant is out of inventory or time elapses)

5. Sales details are delivered to crafter

6. Any remaining product is returned to crafter

This is still a high-level flow, and it should definitely not be confused with the actual set of events and aggregates to be used in the application. At least one more level of translation needs to be done. The consignment flow on page 156 shows what I came up with.

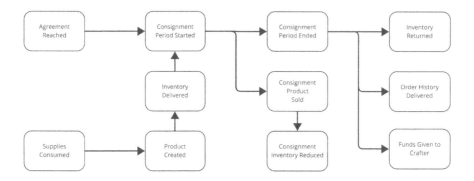

One of the key things about this diagram is that it still isn't something that resembles an event sourcing design. This diagram doesn't capture all the subtleties. For example, the consignment period cannot begin until the crafter has delivered the inventory. Further, some events in this flow might not actually make it into the real event sourcing model. It may not matter to the application when each individual sale of a product took place and the inventory was reduced since a complete report of transactions is available at the end of the consignment period.

Iterate on the Model Document

Iterating on the model document can be deceptively difficult. Non-technical SMEs should probably not be directly involved in this except for further interviews. I made this mistake and ended up in a long (and unnecessary) conversation about when an order starts. I was convinced that it started before determining the order type, whether it's a custom order or a point-of-sale order. The SME, naturally, had a much more user-centric view of things, saying that *"orders start when they start."* We were both right, of course, and I'd unnecessarily confused the situation by trying to get the SME to reason about the world using my internal perspective, not theirs.

Finalizing the event sourcing model requires translation, awareness of multiple viewpoints on the same problem, and the common vocabulary you've hopefully already established.

Build the App

The final truth of this case study is that the event model is never actually finished, it's simply rich enough to allow the developer to start coding. We know event models evolve and thankfully we're already prepared to deal with that.

After having read this book and gone through the motions of converting event models into real code, this should be the easy part, right? I've started the event model docs for Crafter Hustle, and I hope to find the time to build the Crafter Hustle app with a link to it and its GitHub repository.[15]

Wrapping Up

In this chapter, you got a taste of the experience, tooling, and ecosystem available to you for modeling your commands, events, and the flow of information through your application. While no single tool or technique is objectively best to use, you should now have enough information to perform your own research and create your own prototypes to evaluate whatever tools and technology look most promising for your needs.

Whatever you choose, make sure that it fits your development style, has low friction with your development iteration cycles, is automation-friendly, and can hopefully create a meaningful synchronization between your code and your model.

Now that you've started working on ways to tackle increasingly complex models, in the next chapter you'll learn some techniques for dealing with applications and models with high scaling demands.

---

15. https://crafterhustle.dev

## CHAPTER 11

Scaling Up and Out

Now that you've explored how to approach more complex modeling, you're ready to tackle scaling things up and out. Scaling an application from your local development environment out to support hundreds of thousands of concurrent requests, optimized for geographic location, with multiple redundancies is another of the many drop-off points where developers building event-sourced applications become frustrated and give up.

The historical difficulty and complexity of this can be daunting or even appear insurmountable. Thankfully, event sourcing dramatically simplifies scaling applications up and out. But it doesn't relieve you from the responsibility of dealing with the different architectural patterns you encounter at scale.

This chapter will walk through a number of common scenarios you'll encounter as you move event-sourced applications from laptops to production and give you the information you need to know what you should implement yourself versus what you should expect frameworks and libraries to solve. You'll begin with eventual consistency and move on to ordering, duplicate processing, and then a practical example of a tool that works well with event sourcing, *NATS*.

While this chapter may help you scale out your event-sourced applications, it is no substitute for a more in-depth discussion of distributed systems. Things that work in single, isolated processes often fail in bizarre ways when moved to a distributed system. We often learn that our monoliths were only working by sheer happenstance, and moving to a distributed paradigm highlighted our mistakes.

Reading Your Writes

In monolithic applications, it's easy to take for granted that we can read the data we've written. When everything is in a single process, reading a projection created by the flow of events through aggregates is easy—just read the data.

But when applications are running at large scales, we can't rely on the level of consistency offered by a monolith. Assume you've written your application as a monolith, and now you're scaling the application out to multiple geographic regions. Your projection database is now replicated from a single replica leader (often unfortunately called the "master"). Your application writes to a local event stream which is then propagated to the cluster leader. Take a look at the following diagram illustrating this pattern:

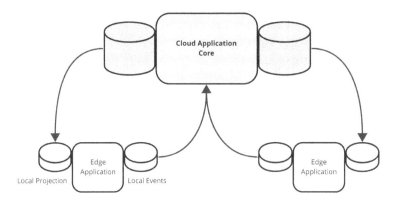

This pattern is extremely common and becoming even more popular as infrastructure that was previously housed within a cloud extends out to the edge. The following user scenario happens frequently and breaks our monolithic assumptions of data locality:

1. The user interacts with a web application cached close to their location.
2. Their actions result in the production of a new event.
3. The event propagates to the cluster leader.
4. *The user reads data from the edge-local projection replica.*
5. The newly updated projection replicates out from the leader to the edge.

In this scenario, the data the user reads after their action produces a write is *inconsistent*. In many cases, this is harmless: after all, many social networking applications have trained users to cope with eventual consistency. But if decisions or further data writes depend on the consistency of the local data, we've got a problem.

Obviously, the easiest way to solve this problem is to *not solve it*. If your application can tolerate this kind of eventual consistency, then embrace it and don't worry. Unfortunately, not everyone is this lucky.

The list of solutions to this problem has no end, and you can spend an eternity with your favorite search engine going down this rabbit hole. One of the simpler solutions, which I call "wait for my writes," can be straightforward to implement.

This solution involves keeping track of the *last sequence number* (*LSN*), though you can also find it called the "highest version," "generation," or even "high watermark." If your application can take note of the revision or version of a particular projection at the time when an event-emitting action takes place, then it can wait until that projection's revision has increased. This allows your application to wait for its own writes...*almost*.

Edge cases like this one keep me up at night. Assume your application has emitted a local event which will work its way through the replication pipeline and come back in the form of a new projection version. If we naively wait for the version to bump by one, then we're not reading *our* writes—we're reading *anyone*'s writes. Any change made by any other user within the cluster can bump this version *before* my application sees its own write.

If we push all of the changes to the cluster leader, then we're just foisting the consistency resolution problem into the cloud instead of the edge. At some point, the conflicts need to be resolved and applications need varying levels of consistency guarantees.

It's worth remembering that projections are merely read models and shouldn't be used for things like the validation logic that aggregates perform. If you can solve this problem by tolerating some level of volatility in your projections, your life will be that much easier. Another common technique is that an application makes the change it expects to see in local data, and then when the replication comes down from the leader, that data wins (or another merge strategy is applied).

If your application cannot tolerate this kind of eventual consistency, then you might need to look into a more heavyweight solution like *Conflict-Free Replicated Data Types* (*CRDTs*),[1] a topic worthy of a book on its own. Rather than implementing these data structures yourself, you might look into products that use them internally like Redis or Riak. The old adage warning you to never implement your own cryptography should also apply to things like CRDTs and consensus algorithms.

---

1. https://en.wikipedia.org/wiki/Conflict-free_replicated_data_type

Remember that you're building an application, not a CRDT framework, so devote your time accordingly.

Preparing for Disorder

In a distributed system, two users interacting with the same application from different origins at the same time will almost never have consistent timing. Sometimes a button press may result in a message being delivered to the backend in milliseconds and other times the message could be lost or take more than a full second to deliver.

Take a close look at your aggregates and process managers before you deploy them at scale. Could they produce different results based on a different ordering of events? If this is the case, then you have a couple of practical options available to help you avoid things becoming nightmarish.

The easiest solution is to change your model such that the order in which your events are processed doesn't matter. If a bank deposit, then withdrawal, and then deposit can all occur in different sequences, then your life will be measurably more tranquil than the alternative.

When you do need to ensure that events are processed in the order in which they are received, see if this is something your event store or message broker can handle for you. You're in the business of building an application, not writing complex algorithms to produce distributed sequences and ensure global ordering. NATS, RabbitMQ, Cassandra, Event Store, Kafka, and many others all have varying levels of control over global ordering and consistency.

The short answer here is to either design your way around the need for predictable ordering or use a tool that takes care of this problem for you. While you *can* use your own algorithms and data structures to attempt to manage global ordering, the truth is that this is a hard problem already solved by (at least for me) people far more skilled at these things.

Another alternative to fixed ordering is using the ideas of *correlation* and *causation*. Ensuring a globally fixed order is often difficult or impossible, but referencing an event that *caused* another event is typically much easier and can be reconciled by the projectors. Even if these events arrive out of order, the causation ID can still be used to establish logical sequence.

If you need to know that two events are related to each other, but order doesn't matter, then you can use *correlation*. A number of popular event sourcing tools and data stores come built-in with support for correlation and causation identifiers.

It's easy to think that you need either correlation or causation (or both). But many times this need is something that your event store needs, and your own higher-level events don't need this. Before you saturate your domain model with correlations and causes, make sure those relations are part of your model and not your infrastructure.

Preventing Duplicate Processing

When reading through the feature lists for message brokers and other event sourcing tools, you'll often see two different phrases: *at-least-once processing* and *at-most-once processing*. If you're lucky, you'll even find systems (like NATS in some situations) that can guarantee *exactly-once processing*.

At-least-once processing means that you're guaranteed to get the one event, but you could also theoretically receive multiple copies of the same event. Some applications and brokers deal with this problem by assigning unique IDs to events and using that ID to remove or ignore duplicates. In other products, you might see a "duplicate window," where some configurable time exists during which the broker will purge messages that are identical to a previously received message within that window. This can be useful when systems producing the events might produce identical events with different IDs.

At-most-once processing means the system guarantees you'll never receive a duplicate message, but it does so at the expense of ensuring a message will always be delivered. In this mode, it's possible and even expected that messages may be lost. In at-most-once environments, clients publishing events often need to perform explicit acknowledgments or handshakes to ensure the processing of a message because the broker doesn't guarantee delivery. This can be useful in environments where you might have an incredibly rapid and large stream of events, but the loss of a few doesn't matter because the system will correct itself on a forthcoming event.

This pattern is common in the IoT world where you might be subscribing to a stream of events from hardware sensors. Loss of a single sensor message is acceptable because you know the sensor will be publishing another message shortly. This is also a pretty typical pattern in other high-traffic environments like gaming backends. Losing a player's position update isn't the end of the world because the client will send another update shortly.

Event Sourcing at Scale with NATS

At its core, NATS is a universal connectivity and messaging system. For those of us old enough to remember the days of landlines, we like to say that NATS is a *universal dial tone*, and the company Synadia provides a global, managed version of this, giving applications cheap access to messaging anywhere in the world.

NATS also supports persistent, replicated streams and additional abstractions built on top of those such as key-value stores and object stores. NATS doesn't require a heavy-handed central administration like some other messaging products and can be used easily on a laptop for testing and clustered globally for production. The durable streams NATS supports are ideal for building event-sourced applications.

In this section, you'll go through the process of creating streams and consumers and use the nats CLI to step through the various application behaviors common to event sourcing.

If you don't have NATS installed and running, take a moment to follow the installation instructions[2] or use the docker image for instant gratification before proceeding.

Once you have the server installed, simply start it up using the default settings but make sure you enable the JetStream feature, which you can do by passing the -js option:

```
$ nats-server -js
```

With your server running, you can now interact with it using the nats CLI. This CLI isn't automatically installed when you install the server, but the installation is also quick and easy (especially if you're a Go developer). Follow the instructions[3] to get the CLI installed before continuing.

NATS streams (which are part of the JetStream feature) are an incredibly powerful tool. They allow you to capture all traffic sent to a set of subjects and then create applications on top of that. You can cluster and mirror streams, send copies of messages from one stream to another, or even use multiple streams as the source of a larger stream. Unlike RabbitMQ and Kafka, we don't need to make some of these partitioning and queue decisions before we get started.

Let's create a stream to hold events for a fictitious application called "LFG Heroes,"[4] an application that works like a matching service to help match players looking for groups with players who want to help. As you can see from the application's event catalog, it revolves around the concept of creating, advancing, and terminating cooperative play sessions.

---

2. https://docs.nats.io/running-a-nats-service/introduction/installation
3. https://github.com/nats-io/natscli#installation
4. https://lfgheroes.com

To create the stream, run nats stream create and answer the prompts as follows:

```
$ nats stream create
[localhost] ? Stream Name EVENTS
[localhost] ? Subjects lfgheroes.events.*
[localhost] ? Storage file
[localhost] ? Replication 1
[localhost] ? Retention Policy Limits
[localhost] ? Discard Policy Old
[localhost] ? Stream Messages Limit -1
[localhost] ? Per Subject Messages Limit -1
[localhost] ? Total Stream Size -1
[localhost] ? Message TTL -1
[localhost] ? Max Message Size -1
[localhost] ? Duplicate tracking time window 2m0s
[localhost] ? Allow message Roll-ups No
[localhost] ? Allow message deletion Yes
[localhost] ? Allow purging subjects or the entire stream Yes
Stream EVENTS was created

Information for Stream EVENTS created 2023-10-01 09:02:48

              Subjects: lfgheroes.events.*
              Replicas: 1
               Storage: File

Options:

             Retention: Limits
        Acknowledgments: true
        Discard Policy: Old
       Duplicate Window: 2m0s
            Direct Get: true
      Allows Msg Delete: true
          Allows Purge: true
        Allows Rollups: false

Limits:

       Maximum Messages: unlimited
   Maximum Per Subject: unlimited
          Maximum Bytes: unlimited
           Maximum Age: unlimited
   Maximum Message Size: unlimited
     Maximum Consumers: unlimited

State:

              Messages: 0
                 Bytes: 0 B
        First Sequence: 0
         Last Sequence: 0
       Active Consumers: 0
```

The first thing worth pointing out in this new stream is that it allows message deletion and stream purging. This should *only* be used for development and experimentation. A real, production event stream acting as the source of truth needs to be immutable.

Once you've got a stream, you can create *consumers*. Think of a consumer as a pointer to a position within a stream. Durable NATS consumers store their state on the NATS server itself. This has a number of powerful advantages that aren't often appreciated until well after the code is running in production.

At the very least, separate consumers means that different services (or aggregates, projectors, and so on) can consume messages from the same stream at a different rate or even consume a different subset of those messages.

This also means that if one consumer crashes over and over while attempting to process a given message (this kind of message is given the rather dark nickname "poison pill"), other consumers remain unaffected.

Before you create a consumer, let's see what happens when you add a message to the stream. For this kind of stream, simply making a request to the stream subject is enough to store the message:

```
$ nats req lfgheroes.events.test_happened '{"hello": "world"}'
09:30:42 Sending request on "lfgheroes.events.test_happened"
09:30:42 Received with rtt 419.167µs
{"stream":"EVENTS", "seq":1}
```

```
$ nats stream view EVENTS
[1] Subject: lfgheroes.events.test_happened Received: 2023-10-01T09:30:42-04:00

{"hello": "world"}

09:30:58 Reached apparent end of data
```

To see how easy and powerful consumers are, let's create two consumers: one interested in this message and one not.

```
$ nats consumer create
[localhost] ? Consumer name TEST_MONITOR
[localhost] ? Delivery target (empty for Pull Consumers)
[localhost] ? Start policy (all, new, last, subject, 1h, msg sequence) all
[localhost] ? Acknowledgment policy explicit
[localhost] ? Replay policy instant
[localhost] ? Filter Stream by subject (blank for all) \
  lfgheroes.events.test_happened
[localhost] ? Maximum Allowed Deliveries -1
[localhost] ? Maximum Acknowledgments Pending 0
[localhost] ? Deliver headers only without bodies No
[localhost] ? Add a Retry Backoff Policy No
[localhost] ? Select a Stream EVENTS
```

```
Information for Consumer EVENTS > TEST_MONITOR created 2023-10-01T09:34:50-04:00
Configuration:

                    Name: TEST_MONITOR
               Pull Mode: true
          Filter Subject: lfgheroes.events.test_happened
          Deliver Policy: All
              Ack Policy: Explicit
                Ack Wait: 30.00s
           Replay Policy: Instant
          Max Ack Pending: 1,000
        Max Waiting Pulls: 512

State:

  Last Delivered Message: Consumer sequence: 0 Stream sequence: 0
     Acknowledgment Floor: Consumer sequence: 0 Stream sequence: 0
         Outstanding Acks: 0 out of maximum 1,000
      Redelivered Messages: 0
      Unprocessed Messages: 1
            Waiting Pulls: 0 of maximum 512
```

Take a look at the line that includes "Unprocessed Messages". Immediately after creating this consumer, there's 1 message waiting to be consumed. To consume it, you'd write code in your application to pull the message, or you can use the nats CLI:

```
$ nats consumer next EVENTS TEST_MONITOR
[09:36:39] subj: lfgheroes.events.test_happened / tries: 1 /
 cons seq: 1 / str seq: 1 / pending: 0

{"hello": "world"}

Acknowledged message

...

$ nats consumer next EVENTS TEST_MONITOR
nats: error: no message received: nats: timeout
```

Asking for the next message gives us the message pending for this consumer. Asking again times out because you've consumed all of the waiting messages.

To get a better feel for how this all comes together, create another consumer:

```
$ nats consumer create
[localhost] ? Consumer name TEST_DONTCARE
[localhost] ? Delivery target (empty for Pull Consumers)
[localhost] ? Start policy (all, new, last, subject, 1h, msg sequence) all
[localhost] ? Acknowledgment policy explicit
[localhost] ? Replay policy instant
```

```
[localhost] ? Filter Stream by subject (blank for all) \
  lfgheroes.events.test_ignored
[localhost] ? Maximum Allowed Deliveries -1
[localhost] ? Maximum Acknowledgments Pending 0
[localhost] ? Deliver headers only without bodies No
[localhost] ? Add a Retry Backoff Policy No
[localhost] ? Select a Stream EVENTS
Information for Consumer EVENTS > TEST_DONTCARE created
  2023-10-01T09:50:42-04:00

Configuration:

                   Name: TEST_DONTCARE
              Pull Mode: true
         Filter Subject: lfgheroes.events.test_ignored
         Deliver Policy: All
             Ack Policy: Explicit
               Ack Wait: 30.00s
          Replay Policy: Instant
        Max Ack Pending: 1,000
      Max Waiting Pulls: 512

State:

  Last Delivered Message: Consumer sequence: 0 Stream sequence: 0
    Acknowledgment Floor: Consumer sequence: 0 Stream sequence: 0
         Outstanding Acks: 0 out of maximum 1,000
      Redelivered Messages: 0
      Unprocessed Messages: 0
             Waiting Pulls: 0 of maximum 512
```

Now you have two consumers, each interested in different messages, and you can play around with nats req and nats consumer next to see the messaging routing in action. The main stream can contain messages in which either of the consumers are interested as well as messages that aren't pending for any consumers. This is exactly the kind of power and flexibility you want when building out event-sourced applications on infrastructure like NATS.

This should give you an idea of how easy it is to use NATS as a substrate to support event-sourced applications. NATS gives you durable streams, durable consumers, and even features like key-value stores and object stores built-in that can be harnessed by event sourcing applications and frameworks. ## Wrapping Up If you found this chapter wasn't nearly as complex as you initially expected it to be, that's excellent. One of the many advantages of an event-sourced application is that if the laws aren't violated and some thought is devoted to modeling and design, scaling out from your laptop to a global application should be relatively easy. You can avoid some common pitfalls by choosing the right message broker and designing your event model with scale and distribution in mind.

As you finish reading this book, I hope you've been inspired by event sourcing's simplicity, surprisingly easy development, and of course, scalability. You can use this inspiration as you start thinking about building your own event-sourced application right now.

APPENDIX 1

The Laws of Event Sourcing

The following is a summary of the laws of event sourcing discussed throughout the book. I have personally violated each one of these laws on past projects and seen the product-breaking consequences firsthand. Some decisions fall into the category of personal or team preference, and others are small architectural deviations, but these are ones I've specifically gathered over time through retrospectives, post-mortems, and production systems engulfed in flame.

A Note from My Lawyers

 My lawyers would like me to tell you that none of these laws are legally binding. But, like an author needs to know the rules of grammar before they can choose which rules to break, the same applies to these.

All Events Are Immutable and Past Tense

Every event represents something that actually happened. An event cannot be modified and always refers to something that took place. Modeling the absence of a thing or a thing that didn't actually occur may often seem like a good idea, but doing so can confuse both developers and event processors. Remember that if an error didn't result in some immutable thing happening, it shouldn't be modeled as an event.

Applying a Failure Event Must Always Return the Previous State

Any attempt to apply a bad, unexpected, or explicitly modeled failure event to an existing state must always return the existing state. Failure events should only indicate that a failed thing occurred in the past, not command rejections.

All Data Required for a Projection Must Be on the Events

The event is the *only* source of truth. If code allows a different piece of information to be supplied as a parameter that contradicts information on the event, you can corrupt an entire event stream. As such, all keys, metadata, and payload data must come from events and nowhere else. This is often one of the hardest laws to follow but the penalties for breaking it can be subtle and disastrous.

Work Is a Side Effect

A frequently asked question in new event sourcing projects is "where does the work happen?" Aggregates aren't allowed to perform side effects or read from external data. Process managers aren't allowed to perform side effects or read from external data. Projectors can create external data, but they can't perform "work" either. If you follow the rule that work is a side effect, things may be easier to understand. If work is a mutation of the world outside the event-sourced system, then work is a side effect, and side effects are only allowed through gateways. The core primitives of aggregates, projectors, and process managers must never do work.

All Projections Must Stem from Events

Every piece of data produced by any projector *must* stem from at least one event. You cannot ever create projection data based on information from outside the event stream. Doing so would violate other event sourcing laws and ruin your system's ability to participate in replays.

Never Manage More than One Flow per Process Manager

Each process manager is responsible for a single, isolated process. Its internal state represents that of an instance of that managed flow (for example, "Order 421," "Batch 73," or "New User Provisioning for User ABC"). As tempting as it may be to create a process manager for "orders" or "users," never lump multiple process flows into a single manager. Doing so generally means the failure of one flow can cascade out throughout the system. Keeping flows separate also avoids accidentally corrupting one process state with that of another.

Process Managers Must Not Read from Projections

It can be tempting to just query from a projection in order for a process manager to gather the information it needs to do its job. This is a dangerous temptation that needs to be resisted. Not only are projections managed by other entities, and are consequently subject to schema change (or outright removal), but in eventually consistent systems, projections won't produce reliably consistent results.

This is one of the hardest laws to follow, and a lot of the arguments for violating it can sound reasonable. Done once, the consequences might seem insignificant, but this pattern permeated throughout a codebase can break consistency and, even worse, violate the predictable nature of replays.

Event Schemas Are Immutable

Event schemas must never change. Any change to an event schema produces a brand-new event type. This means that each new version of an event is a unique type.

Different Projectors Cannot Share Projections

Projectors must share nothing with other projectors. They're free to update their own data but can neither read nor write projections managed by other projectors.

Never Test Internal State

Internal state of aggregates and process managers can change in form and purpose. Tests should supply input and assert output without enforcing or asserting the shape of internal state.

Index

Thank you!

We hope you enjoyed this book and that you're already thinking about what you want to learn next. To help make that decision easier, we're offering you this gift.

Head on over to https://pragprog.com right now, and use the coupon code BUYANOTHER2025 to save 30% on your next ebook. Offer is void where prohibited or restricted. This offer does not apply to any edition of *The Pragmatic Programmer* ebook.

And if you'd like to share your own expertise with the world, why not propose a writing idea to us? After all, many of our best authors started off as our readers, just like you. With up to a 50% royalty, world-class editorial services, and a name you trust, there's nothing to lose. Visit https://pragprog.com/become-an-author/ today to learn more and to get started.

Thank you for your continued support. We hope to hear from you again soon!

The Pragmatic Bookshelf

Practical Microservices

MVC and CRUD make software easier to write, but harder to change. Microservice-based architectures can help even the smallest of projects remain agile in the long term, but most tutorials meander in theory or completely miss the point of what it means to be microservice based. Roll up your sleeves with real projects and learn the most important concepts of evented architectures. You'll have your own deployable, testable project and a direction for where to go next.

Ethan Garofolo
(290 pages) ISBN: 9781680506457. $45.95
https://pragprog.com/book/egmicro

Serverless Apps on Cloudflare

Use serverless technologies to build applications that scale, more quickly and easily, and without worrying about deployment. Whether you're writing an API, a full-stack app, or real-time code, harness the power of serverless on Cloudflare's platform so you can focus on what you do best: delivering solutions. With hands-on instruction and code samples throughout, you'll go from building a simple API to analyzing images with AI. And, when it's time to launch, you'll learn how to deploy your applications and websites automatically, and how to optimize their performance for production.

Ashley Peacock
(275 pages) ISBN: 9798888650714. $53.95
https://pragprog.com/book/apapps

Test-Driven React, Second Edition

Turn your React project requirements into tests and
get the feedback you need faster than ever before.
Combine the power of testing, linting, and typechecking
directly in your coding environment to iterate on React
components quickly and fearlessly!

Trevor Burnham
(172 pages) ISBN: 9798888650653. $45.95
https://pragprog.com/book/tbreact2

A Common-Sense Guide to Data Structures and Algorithms in Python, Volume 1

If you thought data structures and algorithms were all
just theory, you're missing out on what they can do
for your Python code. Learn to use Big O notation to
make your code run faster by orders of magnitude.
Choose from data structures such as hash tables,
trees, and graphs to increase your code's efficiency
exponentially. With simple language and clear diagrams, this book makes this complex topic accessible,
no matter your background. Every chapter features
practice exercises to give you the hands-on information
you need to master data structures and algorithms for
your day-to-day work.

Jay Wengrow
(502 pages) ISBN: 9798888650356. $57.95
https://pragprog.com/book/jwpython

Your Code as a Crime Scene, Second Edition

Jack the Ripper and legacy codebases have more in common than you'd think. Inspired by forensic psychology methods, you can apply strategies to identify problems in your existing code, assess refactoring direction, and understand how your team influences the software architecture. With its unique blend of criminal psychology and code analysis, *Your Code as a Crime Scene* arms you with the techniques you need to take on any codebase, no matter what programming language you use.

Adam Tornhill
(336 pages) ISBN: 9798888650325. $53.95
https://pragprog.com/book/atcrime2

Creating Software with Modern Diagramming Techniques

Diagrams communicate relationships more directly and clearly than words ever can. Using only text-based markup, create meaningful and attractive diagrams to document your domain, visualize user flows, reveal system architecture at any desired level, or refactor your code. With the tools and techniques this book will give you, you'll create a wide variety of diagrams in minutes, share them with others, and revise and update them immediately on the basis of feedback. Adding diagrams to your professional vocabulary will enable you to work through your ideas quickly when working on your own code or discussing a proposal with colleagues.

Ashley Peacock
(156 pages) ISBN: 9781680509830. $29.95
https://pragprog.com/book/apdiag

The Pragmatic Bookshelf

The Pragmatic Bookshelf features books written by professional developers for professional developers. The titles continue the well-known Pragmatic Programmer style and continue to garner awards and rave reviews. As development gets more and more difficult, the Pragmatic Programmers will be there with more titles and products to help you stay on top of your game.

Visit Us Online

This Book's Home Page
https://pragprog.com/book/khpes
Source code from this book, errata, and other resources. Come give us feedback, too!

Keep Up-to-Date
https://pragprog.com
Join our announcement mailing list (low volume) or follow us on Twitter @pragprog for new titles, sales, coupons, hot tips, and more.

New and Noteworthy
https://pragprog.com/news
Check out the latest Pragmatic developments, new titles, and other offerings.

Save on the ebook

Save on the ebook versions of this title. Owning the paper version of this book entitles you to purchase the electronic versions at a terrific discount.

PDFs are great for carrying around on your laptop—they are hyperlinked, have color, and are fully searchable. Most titles are also available for the iPhone and iPod touch, Amazon Kindle, and other popular e-book readers.

Send a copy of your receipt to support@pragprog.com and we'll provide you with a discount coupon.

Contact Us

Online Orders:	*https://pragprog.com/catalog*
Customer Service:	*support@pragprog.com*
International Rights:	*translations@pragprog.com*
Academic Use:	*academic@pragprog.com*
Write for Us:	*http://write-for-us.pragprog.com*